SIX PLAYS
OF THE YIDDISH THEATRE

SIX PLAYS OF THE YIDDISH THEATRE

By

DAVID PINSKI — SHOLOM ASH
PEREZ HIRSCHBEIN — SOLOMON J. RABINOWITSCH

Translated and Edited by
ISAAC GOLDBERG, PH. D.

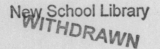
BOSTON
JOHN W. LUCE AND COMPANY

Printed in U. S. A.

PUBLISHER'S NOTE

THE plays offered to the English reading public in this volume are not presented as the crowning achievement of a national stage which is ready to assume its place among the great theatres of the world. The purpose of their publication is rather to show the present stage of development in a dramatic literature which bids fair to give articulate expression to the esthetic sense of a widely scattered people whose social isolation has preserved to them traditions, customs and habits of thought which, with but slight variation, have persisted from the earliest period of recorded history and are alien to the people among whom they dwell.

Drama springing from such a source naturally limits itself at the outset to the rather elastic class of compositions designated as "folk plays," in which a simple motivation is employed to depict incidents of daily life and characters drawn from the common types familiar to author and audience alike.

The Yiddish Theatre while presenting some of its most characteristic work in that class of drama has in addition a background of Oriental and Biblical tradition rich in poetic imagery, from

which its playwriters draw with a sympathy and
felicity that is strikingly effective.

Unlike the recent dramatic movement in Ireland
with which all students of the stage are familiar,
the Yiddish Theatre has produced no masterpiece
comparable with, say "Riders to the Sea," nor can
it boast a dramatist that the commending genius
of Synge does not overtop. But on the other
hand while the Irish Theatre considered as a whole
never gave promise of becoming more than a
reflection of local characteristics and after a short
period of brilliant creation, within very narrow
limits to be sure, came to a dead halt, the Yiddish
Stage shows every evidence of a tendency to so
broaden its scope as ultimately to establish a well
balanced drama of permanent vitality that will
find its place in the great stream of drama the
current of which flows through the literature of all
intellectual peoples.

The reader should bear in mind the peculiar
difficulties under which this attempt at dramatic
expression has labored from the start, the limited
vision of an uneducated audience, and particularly
the absence of a dramatic stage tradition among
the Jews,—a matter of great significance to a people
whose life is much influenced by tradition.

It should be remembered also that the deep,
often terrible significance, associated with the
observance or infraction of certain religious customs

affords Yiddish dramatists a means of producing intensely dramatic effects that would be entirely lost on an audience or reader not familiar with their meaning.

In brief these plays, several of them somewhat crude, are representative of a dramatic movement in its making, a stage of development perhaps of greater interest to the student of the drama than one in which the ultimate possibilities of development have been reached, giving as it does an opportunity to forecast the branches that will expand their buds and blossom, and those that will shrivel up, blacken, and in the end fall to the ground to lose themselves in the litter.

And yet, notwithstanding these crudities one may search far for a bit of drama more suggestive, in composition and color, of a nocturne by Blakelock or Whistler than is "The Sinner," or a piece of more florid tone, drawn in with more sweeping curves and with a broader line than in the fine Biblical drama of "Abigail."

CONTENTS

DAVID PINSKI

By reason of the chaste art, the modern technique and the pregnant vision of his best plays, David Pinski is entitled to be considered the most significant of contemporary Jewish dramatists. In him the satiric spirit of Goldfaden and the theatrical talents of Jacob Gordin are fused in an artistry greater than that attained by either of his noted predecessors; he represents the latest and best phase of the rapid and irregular evolution of the Jewish drama since the foundation of the Yiddish stage, in Roumania, in 1876 by Abraham Goldfaden.

Pinski was born at Mobilov, Russia, in 1872. Early moving to Moscow, he was forced to leave in 1892 at the time of the expulsion of the Jews. Proceeding to Warsaw, he began to write the stories of proletarian life in the Russian ghetto which first brought him recognition. Pinski soon went to Berlin for study. In 1899 he came to New York to assume the duties of literary editor upon a Socialist weekly. He has also been a student at Columbia University.

"Like all the more notable masters of the modern theatre," says Ludwig Lewisohn, "he started out as a consistent naturalist, embodying in *Eisik*

Scheftel' and in other plays the struggle and tragedy of the Jewish proletariat; like them he has, in later years, cultivated vision and imagination in '*The Eternal Jew*' and '*The Dumb Messiah*' and a series of exquisite plays in one act dealing with the loves of King David. These plays are written in a rhythmic prose created by Pinski himself. That prose is as subtly beautiful as Maeterlinck's or Yeats'; in passion and reality the Jewish playwright surpasses both."

Among the better known of Pinski's longer plays is "The Treasure", produced in Berlin (1910) in a German translation, by Max Rheinhardt. The theme of the play is money. But whereas money, in Gordin's great play, "God, Man and Devil", is viewed as a corruptive power against which man's better self instinctively revolts, here it is looked upon as being only incidentally the root of all evil, and potentially a boon to the possessor. For one day, at least, Tillie's soap-bubble reputation as a millionairess brings her the sweetest fruits of riches. To taste these she desecrates the holiest day in the calendar, while the villagers, in their attempt to find the source of Tillie's suddenly acquired wealth, rake over the stones of the cemetery until they wake the dead.

Pinski's work as a critic represents some of the best that Yiddish drama has called forth. His little pamphlet, *Dos Yiddishe Drama*, is a series of articles on the history of the Jewish stage which is of far greater importance than its modest form would seem to indicate; his discussion of Jacob Gordin is exceptionally illuminating.

Of Pinski's work this volume presents two one-act dramas, *Abigail* and *Forgotten Souls*.

Abigail, although complete in itself, is one of the beautiful series of one-act plays based upon the loves of King David. The story of Abigail may be found in I Samuel, XXV. In many cases the dramatist employs the language of the Bible, word for word, so that in translation I have used the corresponding passages in the St. James version. In others the Biblical passage is slightly altered.

A comparison of the Biblical chapter with Pinski's dramatization throws interesting light upon the playwright's art. The characters are true to history, and the words of the Biblical narrative often acquire added meaning through the dramatist's interpolations.

From the standpoint of absolute technique *Abigail* may be said to represent as high a mark as has been reached in Yiddish drama.

The original title of *"Forgotten Souls"* is *"Gluecks-Vergessene,"* i. e., those who have been forgotten, or overlooked, by happiness. The theme of the self-sacrificing sister is common to the Yiddish stage, even as the sacrifice of self for others is common in Yiddish life. The development of the play is accomplished with the dramatic power, restraint and truth to life which has given Pinski the leading position he occupies among Jewish dramatists.

ABIGAIL

A Biblical Drama in One Act

By DAVID PINSKI

PERSONS.

DAVID.

NABAL, *Abigail's husband*.

ABISHUR, *the priest*.

AHIMELECH.

A *Servant of Abigail's Suite*.

ABIGAIL.

JOAB
ABISHAI } *sons of Zeruiah, David's sister*.
ASAHEL

A *Servant of Nabal's Suite*.

David's Men; Vassals of Abigail and Nabal.

6

ABIGAIL

A Biblical Drama in One Act

SCENE: *David's camp, in a rocky spot of the Wilderness of Paran. David, his sword across his knee, is seated upon a stone in the center. In front of him, upon the earth, sit Abishur and Ahimelech. Asahel, stretched before David, almost touches with his head the knees of the leader. Around and about, in various postures, are David's men, — exhausted, famished, with the burning noonday sun playing down upon them. All eyes are turned toward the left, in tense expectation.*

ASAHEL.

[*To Ahimelech, stretching out his closed fists.*]

Guess which hand containeth the stone. If thou divinest rightly, then hath Nabal granted our request; if not, then hath he made light of David's words.

AHIMELECH.

[*Ill-humoredly.*]

And will that still mine hunger?

ASAHEL.

It is but a pastime. If thy stomach be angry, appease it with play. Thou wilt not guess? — Hm ! — Priest Abishur, thou ? Thou art indeed a diviner.

ABISHUR.

Hold bread in thy fists, then would I guess correctly.

ASAHEL.

A mouse could do that better. Ah ! Ye are an ill-humored tribe; there is no playing with ye. [*Turns to David.*] Why sittest so distraught, mine uncle ? What thinkest thou ? Whither fly thy thoughts ? Broodest thou over the past ? Or art thou piercing the future ? — To behold thee in thought is my pleasure. I have no thoughts of mine own, so would I fain guess yours. And I sit and ponder, and ponder . . .

DAVID.
[*In subdued laughter.*]

Ha-Ha !

ASAHEL.

Wert thou thinking of Saul ? Or of Jonathan ? Or — or of Michal, thy wife ? — Oh ! I have offended thee ! — Perhaps thou wouldst have thy harp ? [*Angry laughter is heard. Asahel mocks*

it.] Ha-ha-ha ! [*To David.*] Sing something.
[*The laughter is repeated.*]

DAVID.

[*Lays his hand with utmost kindness upon
Asahel's head.*]

JOAB.

Better ask him to gird his sword. He should
have followed my advice from the very beginning.
Instead of sending ten of us, all of us should have
gone, and instead of sending to Nabal a request,
we should have made our point with our lances.
Had we done so, we would not now be sitting,
listening to the music of our empty stomachs.

[*Murmuring of the men.*]

Certainly — Naturally — He speaketh justly.

JOAB.

No asking for things, say I.   One should never
ask.

AHIMELECH.

It would have been better had we sent to his
wife. She, so they say, is as good as she is beautiful. But he, — he is an unworthy wretch.

ASAHEL.

He will not dare to refuse us after the boons he hath received from our hands.

JOAB.

Ha-ha-ha ! . . . Saul, too, received boons from our hands, and continuously, yet did he — Ha-ha-ha ! And here we are, stranded in the wilderness of Paran, suffering from hunger and from thirst. There was a time when, if we had ceased to play our role as benefactors, we would now be serving the king of Judea.

DAVID.

[Sternly.]

Joab !

[Murmuring of the men.]

The king of Judea — Yea, the king of Judea!

DAVID.

That word must be forgotten ! As long as he liveth, Saul is our king, nor I nor any that be true to me shall harm a hair of his head. He is the anointed of God. The son of Zeruiah believeth that he is true to me and loveth me when he speaketh of kingdom. Little doth he know how grievously he insulteth.

JOAB.

We shall never understand one another.

DAVID.

Then keep silence, and learn to understand me.

JOAB.

Then explain to me, why the ten messengers to Nabal ? For he is not Saul, the anointed of God. Why the soft speech and the prayerful language ? "Peace be both to thee, and peace be to thine house, and peace be unto all that thou hast ! " . . Fie !

DAVID.

King wouldst thou have me of Judea, yet askest that I stoop to robbery.

JOAB.

Comport thyself like a king ! Give orders ! Rule ! Command !

DAVID.

[Sternly.]

Then I command thee to keep silence. Rouse not the impatience of the men.

ASAHEL.

I should have gone. Thou shouldst have sent me, the fleet of foot. Then had I long returned hither.

[*Voices from the left.*]

They come ! They come ! — They come empty-handed !

JOAB.

Ha-ha-ha !

DAVID.

Empty hand — [*Seizes his sword, arises, and shouts to the returning messengers.*] Faster, I say ! I must know the answer immediately !

[*Voices.*]

Faster ! David must know the answer immediately !

ABISHAI.

[*Advances from the left with his men.*]

DAVID.

Ye return empty-handed.

ABISHAI.

As thou beholdest.

DAVID.

Hath he perhaps sent something after ye ?

ABISHAI.

His scorn.

DAVID.

Then surely must thou in some manner have insulted him. Thou couldst not restrain thy bitter tongue, and before thou hadst opened thy mouth to speak, thou must have lost thy patience. Thou art after all a brother to Joab.

ABISHAI.

My companions are my witnesses. I delivered to him thy request word for word, even as thou gavest it to me. Over the whole way did I repeat it to myself, schooling myself in the task of prayerful request. Not a word of thine did I omit — my companions are my witnesses — nor did I add a single word. They can corroborate me. I did not lose my patience, not even when he insulted thee and us. Speak I the truth, friends?

COMPANIONS.

The very truth !

ABISHAI.

We did not have our swords with us. Thou tookest them from us.

DAVID.

[Impatiently.]

Tell the story !

ABISHAI.

I said to him: "We come to thee with a greeting of peace from David, son of Jesse." His sour visage became more sour, but I bethought me of thy counsel, nor did my voice continue in the least less friendly. "Thus hath David ordered us to speak: Long life to thee [*A murmur of resentment among the men*] and peace be both to thee, and peace be to thine house, and peace be to all that thou hast."

JOAB.

[*Laughs derisively.*]

ABISHAI.

"And now I have heard that thou shearest thy sheep; now thy shepherds which were with us, we hurt them not, neither was there ought missing to them, all the while they were in Carmel. Ask thy young men and they will show thee. Wherefore let my young men find favor in thine eyes; for we come in a good day. Give, I pray thee, whatsoever cometh to thy hand unto thy servants and to thy son David."

JOAB.

"Thy son David ! Thy son David !"

ABISHAI.

Thus spake I unto him, word for word, and in the most abject prayerful manner. [*To his companions.*] Is it not true ?

A Companion.

We burned with shame, so beggarly was his demeanor.

Abishai.

[Between his teeth.]

And oh ! how it boiled within me!

David.

[Impatient.]

And then ?

Abishai.

He turned away from us, and with angry scorn, departed.

David.

[Raising his sword.]

Abishai.

Now cometh the worst. We lay down upon the earth and resolved to wait for a clearer and more wordy reply. And lo — the reply came. We had well rested ourselves from our journey, and he, no longer able to endure the sight of us, came in great anger and shouted wildly: "Who is David, and who is the son of Jesse ? There be many servants nowadays that break away every man from his master !"

JOAB.

What ! And he spake thus ?

ABISHAI.

"Shall I then take my bread, and my water, and my flesh that I have killed for my shearers and give it unto men, whom I know not whence they be ?

[*Stops suddenly.*]

DAVID.

[*Hoarsely.*]

Well, continue !

ABISHAI.

That is all. He left us, and we — obeyed thee. We departed without punishing him. — But we have our swords —

DAVID.

[*With the full strength of his voice.*]

Gird ye on every man his sword ! [*Commotion in the camp. David's command is heard repeated along the lines, and there is a noise of swords. David, girding on his sword, to Joab.*] Four hundred come with me, and two hundred remain on guard. Choose the stronger, those who have suffered less from exhaustion and hunger, and let them here remain.

JOAB.

What canst thou mean by this ? Thy command is quite the reverse of reason.

DAVID.

Thou wilt never understand me. Those who have most suffered from exhaustion and hunger must be the first to eat.

JOAB.

[Tapping his forehead.]

I see ! [*Turning to Abishai, Ahimelech and Abishur.*] Come, let us choose those for the expedition and those for the guard.

> [*Joab and the three to whom he has spoken are soon lost among the soldiers.*]

DAVID.

Not a vestige shall remain of him or his. They shall all die !

ASAHEL.

Even his beautiful wife ?

DAVID.

Death ! Death ! Men and women alike, so that not even a memory of him shall remain ! The very place which witnessed his insult to me must

be raized and devastated ! Death ! Death!
Death to every creature and every thing !

[Voices.]

A caravan approacheth ! Behold ! A caravan !

JOAB.

[Hurrying forward.]

A caravan of asses, laden with food, cometh this
way —

DAVID.

Let it pass through ! Let it pass on ! Let no
man dare to touch it ! Today we shall sate ourselves with Nabal's blood and possessions.

SEVERAL SERVANTS.

*[Run up and prostrate themselves before
David.]*

DAVID.

Who are these ?

ABISHUR.

Heralds of the caravan.

DAVID.

Arise, and go your way in peace.

YOUNG MAN.

We have run ahead to apprize thee that our
mistress cometh.

DAVID.

Your mistress ? Who is your mistress ? Cometh
she to me ?

YOUNG MAN.

To thee.   She is Abigail, the wife of Nabal.

DAVID.

How now ! Away from me ! Take them away
from me ! Spare them not !

[*Turns away.*]

THE YOUNG MEN.

[*Kneel before David, clasping his clothes and
wailing. David's men are about to tear
them away.*]

DAVID.

[*Turning again to the young men.*]

Surely in vain have I kept all that this fellow
hath in the wilderness, so that nothing was missed
of all that pertained unto him; and he hath re-
quited me evil for good.

ABIGAIL.

[*Enters, riding upon an ass.*]

DAVID.

[*Does not notice her, and speaks in an acrid
voice to the vassals before him.*]

So and more also do God unto the enemies of
David, if I leave of all that pertain to him by the
morning light a single living creature . . [*Suddenly
notices Abigail, and stops as if smitten with her
beauty, ending his sentence in a confused, low voice*]
. . . a . . . single . . . male . . . creature.

> [*The men about him notice David's features
> and his confusion. They look around,
> behold Abigail, and walk off, releasing her
> servants, who rush to her for protection.
> Silence.*]

>> ABIGAIL.
> [*Descends from the ass, and prostrates herself
>   before David's feet.*]

>> DAVID.
>> [*Withdraws from her.*]

>> ABIGAIL.
> [*Approaches him once more. Oppressive
>   silence.*]

>> JOAB.
>> [*Commanding suddenly.*]

>> ABIGAIL.
> [*Quickly rising upon her knees, stretching
>   her hands imploringly to David.*]

>> DAVID.
>> [*With ironic laughter.*]

Indeed !

ABIGAIL.

Let thine handmaid, I pray thee, speak in thine
audience. Hear, I pray, the words of thine handmaid !

DAVID.

Nabal must die !

ABIGAIL.

Let not my lord, I pray thee, regard this man of
Belial, even Nabal: for as his name is, so is he.
Nabal is his name and folly is with him.   Couldst
thou have expected aught else from him ? Couldst
thou have awaited from him other than a denial ?
But I —

DAVID.

Hast thou too insulted my men and sent them
away empty-handed ?

ABIGAIL.

Oh, my lord ! As the Lord liveth and as thy
soul liveth, and as the Lord hath more than once
withholden thee from shedding blood, and from
avenging thyself with thine own hand. Was
not Saul in thy hands ?

DAVID.

The King !

ABIGAIL.

Oh, my lord! Thy greatest enemy, yet didst thou not kill him. Now let thine other enemies, and they that seek evil to thee, have no greater worth than Nabal.

DAVID.

I must stamp out the vermin.

ABIGAIL.

See the gift which thy handmaid hath brought to her lord: let it be given unto the young men that serve thee.

DAVID.

Thou wouldst bribe me? Wouldst wipe away mine insult with thy gift?

ABIGAIL.

Oh, forgive the trespass of thy handmaid: for the Lord will certainly make my lord a sure house; because my lord fighteth the battles of the Lord, and evil hath not been found in thee all thy days.

DAVID.

I do no evil when I punish.

ABIGAIL.

Oh, leave that to God! And should a man arise to pursue thee, and to seek thy soul, the soul of

Abigail

my lord will be bound in the bundle of life with
the Lord thy God; and the souls of thine enemies,
them shall he sling out as out of the middle of
a sling.

DAVID.
What manner of speech is this ?

ABIGAIL.
And it shall come to pass, when the Lord shall
have done to my lord according to all the good
that he hath spoken concerning thee, and shall
have appointed thee ruler over Israel, that this
shall be no grief unto thee either that thou hast
shed blood causeless or that my lord hath avenged
himself with his own hand. And God shall deal
well with thee and thou wilt remember thine handmaid.

> [*Falls prostrate before David, with arms ex-
> tended. Her servants, in great fright,
> approach with subdued wailing.*]

DAVID.
> [*About to raise Abigail.*]

ASAHEL.
> [*Anticipating David, raises Abigail to her
> knees, puts her arm about his neck and
> helps her to her feet.*]

JOAB.

Our men are waiting, David.   I go with them.

DAVID.

[*Does not reply, nor does he remove his gaze
from Abigail.*]

ABIGAIL.

[*Trembling at Joab's words, opens wide her
eyes and looks at David in mute appeal.*]

DAVID.

[*After regarding her silently.*]

Thou wast not — sent —

ABIGAIL.

[*Raises her hands to him in fright.*]

DAVID.

Thou sayest that — thou wouldst — have me —

ABIGAIL.

[*About to kneel before him again.*]

ASAHEL.

[*Prevents her.*]

DAVID.

[*After regarding Abigail in silence.*]

Blessed be the Lord God of Israel which sent
thee this day to meet me, and blessed be thy advice,

and blessed be thou, which hast kept me this day
from coming to shed blood and from avenging
myself with mine own hand.

ABIGAIL.

[*Relieved and happy.*]

Oh, My lord !

DAVID.

For in very deed, as the Lord God of Israel
liveth, which hath kept me back from hurting
thee, except thou hadst hasted and come to meet
me, surely there had not been left unto Nabal by
the morning light a single . . . a single . . . male
creature.

ABIGAIL.

[*Lowers her eyes, with a sigh of relief.*]

Blessed be God ! — [*Raises her eyes to David.*]
Wilt thou now accept my gift ?

DAVID.

With thanks.

ABIGAIL.

Two hundred loaves of bread have I brought —
will they suffice ? For I knew not how great was
the number of thy men — and two bottles of wine
— surely will they not be enough. Five sheep

ready dressed, five measures of parched corn, an hundred clusters of raisins and two hundred cakes of figs. This is all that I could in my haste have placed upon the asses.

DAVID.

It will suffice. [*Calls out.*] Soldiers! There is what to eat ! Prepare your meal !

> [*Amid cries of "Food ! Food !" the men make towards the left, in the direction of the asses.*]

JOAB.

> [*Angrily.*]

Wise Nabal ! With this little would he save his all !

ABIGAIL.

> [*Frightened, to David.*]

Oh, my lord, I swear unto thee that Nabal knoweth not of a single loaf of bread, nor doth he suspect that I am with thee.

DAVID.

I believe thee. Thou needst not fear. Joab grumbleth because the affair hath passed without bloodshed. [*To Joab.*] Go slake thy thirst with wine. Mayst have my share too.

JOAB.

[*Going.*]

And thou, with what are thou sated ?

ASAHEL.

[*Following Joab.*]

Soon am I too quite sated.

DAVID.

[*Looks at Abigail intensely.*]

ABIGAIL.

[*Lowers her eyes in embarrassment.*]

DAVID.

I have no seat to offer thee, no carpet. I sat but now upon this stone. Wilst thou not seat thyself there ?

ABIGAIL.

Let my lord be seated. His handmaid will stand before him. But thou art hungry; what wilt thou have, that I may serve thee ?

DAVID.

I am sated, since my men have what to eat — and I am sated, since — But be seated, pray, and I shall lie at thy feet. Be seated, else must I stand. — Wait. I shall take off my covering and spread it out upon the stone —

ABIGAIL.

Oh, nay, my lord — thou needst not trouble thyself — I must be journeying back.

DAVID.

[*Spreading his covering of hide over the stone.*]

But — but — thou wilt not journey back straightway. Thou must wait until thine asses have been unburdened, and thou, too, must rest thyself. Or am I unwelcome in thine eyes, and fearest thou me ?

ABIGAIL.

Oh, my lord. I would merely reach home as quickly as may be, lest Nabal —

DAVID.

Recall not Nabal's name to me lest it recall mine anger. Come, be seated.

> [*Takes her by the hand and seats her down upon the stone. He stretches himself out at her feet and gazes up at her most intensely.*]

ABIGAIL.

[*Sits shyly, at a loss, looking about with nervous glances which rest now and then upon David. She would look well at him, but dares not.*]

DAVID.

[*Breaks the oppressive silence, speaking slowly.*]
Thou art called Abigail, then ?

ABIGAIL.

Yea, my lord.

DAVID.

[*Almost to himself, lingering fondly upon the
       word.*]
A — bi — gail. [*Pause.*]   Abigail !

ABIGAIL.

What, my lord ?

DAVID.

What a fair sound hath thy name !

ABIGAIL.

[*Smiling.*]

I am happy that my name pleaseth thee.

DAVID,

Thy name and thy —
              [*Gazes upon her passionately.*]

ABIGAIL.

              [*Her eyelids drooping.*]

DAVID.

[*Suddenly.*]

Tell me, lovest thou thy husband ?

ABIGAIL.

[*In utter conjusion, about to rise.*]

DAVID.

[*Holds her back.   Pause.*]

Dost thou love him ?

ABIGAIL.

[*Finally, in a voice scarcely audible.*]

He is my husband.

DAVID.

You said, before, he was an evil person.

ABIGAIL.

My parents gave me to him to wife.

DAVID.

And thou lovest him not. — Why should I not
indeed punish him ? He hath earned his death.

ABIGAIL.

[*Frightened.*]

Oh !

DAVID.

How now ? Thou lovest him, then !

ABIGAIL.

He is my husband.

DAVID.

Ha-ha !

ABIGAIL.

And my lord must not deign to notice such enemies.

DAVID.

One steppeth upon worms.

ABIGAIL.

Nay ! Do not kill him ! Do not kill him !

DAVID.

Ha-ha ! And now, truly, how hast thou dared to come to me ?

ABIGAIL.

I knew that thou couldst forgive thine enemies.

DAVID.

And what if I should not let thee return ?

ABIGAIL.

[*Jumps up, in terror.*]

Oh, my lord !

DAVID.

Why should Nabal possess so precious a jewel ?
How cometh to such a churl so fair a wife ?

ABIGAIL.

Oh, thou wilt release me !

DAVID.

To return to thine evil husband ?

ABIGAIL.

To my husband. Oh, thou wilt not strive
against God and disobey his holy injunctions.

DAVID.

[*Buries his face in his hands*]

ABIGAIL.

Thou art the Lord's faithful servant and wilt
not do violence to the wife of a stranger.

DAVID.

[*Arising.*]

Thou art right.   Go in peace to thy home.

ABIGAIL.

[Bows very low.]

DAVID.

[Smiling sadly.]

See, I obey thee in all things, and treat thee honorably.

ABIGAIL.

[Again bowing very low.]

Never shall I forget it.

[They regard each other with sad, wistful countenance. Silence.]

DAVID.

Or forget me, either ?

ABIGAIL.

[Her head droops, she blushes, and she is about to leave. There is a commotion to the left, Abigail's servant runs up to her, followed by Asahel and others.]

SERVANT.

Oh, mistress. Thy husband Nabal approacheth !

ABIGAIL.

[Trembling.]

Woe is me !

DAVID.

Thou art under my protection.

ABIGAIL.

He must not find me here.

DAVID.

So much dost thou fear him?

ABIGAIL.

Nay. For his health I fear, and for his life. Stout he is, and full-blooded. Should he see me here and learn what I have done with his possessions, it can make him ill, it can kill him.

DAVID.

If he cometh hither, then will he learn it straightway.

ABIGAIL.

Oh, where can I conceal myself? Oh, let him not see me and deny me! Hide from his eyes my gift!

DAVID.

[*To the servant.*]

How far is Nabal yet from here? I see him not yet upon the way.

SERVANT.

He is still far off. I ran ahead.

DAVID.

[*To Asahel.*]

Run through the ranks of our men and command them to stop eating and drinking. Hide all the food and conceal Nabal's servants among your ranks, and when Nabal arrives let all lie as if in utmost exhaustion, and let him pass through without harm to a hair of his head.

ASAHEL.

Rely upon me. The game will be well played.
[*Leaves together with the servant and the others.*]

DAVID.

[*To Abigail.*]

Conceal thyself behind the stone. He will not see thee.

ABIGAIL.

[*Obeying him.*]

Oh ! Already I behold him ! Seest thou ? That stout fellow who rideth before all the servants.

DAVID.

[*Sitting down upon the stone.*]

He sitteth not sure upon his mount. I could swear the churl is drunken.

ABIGAIL.

And well you may. That is he oft, indeed.

DAVID.

[*Bending down towards her.*]

And that is thy husband ?

ABIGAIL.

Thus hath God willed.

DAVID.

And it is for his life thou tremblest ?

ABIGAIL.

Ever have I shielded his life.

DAVID.

Thou faithful soul ! — — And how fair thou art ! — — Hide thee not yet. He is still far distant. Let me behold thee. — Thus. — Quiet. Be not so afraid. — Quiet. Quiet. — He is still far off. — How fair thou art.

ABIGAIL.

[*With a sudden cry.*]

Oh !

[*Rushes to hide herself.*]

DAVID.

[*Intercepting her.*]

Nay. Hide thee not yet. He is still far off, as thou canst see. Or wouldst thou hide thy beauty ?

[*Gazes at her intently.*]

ABIGAIL.
[*Hides her face on the stone.*]

DAVID.
Abigail.   Let Nabal die.

ABIGAIL.
[*Frightened.*]

Oh, my lord !   Nay !

DAVID.
Abigail, look at me.

ABIGAIL.
[*Her eyes lowered.*]
I wish no guilt in his death. — Oh ! He draws
near ! Oh, swear to me that thou wilt harm him
not !

DAVID.
[*After a long pause.*]

I swear it.

ABIGAIL.
How can I thank thee ! — He must not discover
me here !

DAVID.
He will not discover thee.

ABIGAIL.

[*Suddenly.*]

Oh ! He hath fallen from the ass ! They pulled him down — your men —

DAVID.

[*Jumping down from the stone.*]

It will cost them dear !

NABAL.

[*Enters, scarcely able to stand upon his feet, surrounded by Asahel, Abishur, Ahimelech and a few others, who bow before him mockingly.*]

ABIGAIL.

[*Hides quickly behind the stone.*]

NABAL.

Beggars ! Hungry dogs ! Locusts upon the field of strangers !

DAVID.

[*To his men, sternly.*]

Did ye pull him down ?

ASAHEL.

Nay. The lord fell off himself. We approached him and asked for something to still our hunger.

He wished to strike us, whereupon he fell. [*Bowing to Nabal.*] My lord did not hurt himself ? My lord hath injured none of his limbs ?

ABISHUR.

Woe to the ass that could not carry his master ! We will stone him !

DAVID.

Let him be !

ASAHEL.

We ask but that the lord give us something to eat, else shall we die of hunger before his very eyes.

NABAL.

Ye should have starved long ago. Naught shall ye receive from me but blows. Away, mongrels ! Chew the earth, if ye will.

ASAHEL AND THE OTHERS.

[*With mock entreaty.*]

Oh, have mercy !

NABAL.

[*Aiming blows at them with his staff.*]

With my staff—straightway shall ye feel Nabal's mercy ! Mercy on robbers and thieves ! Ha-ha ! . . . I'll strike thee once, and twice . . . [*They run away from him,*   *He pursues them, then turns back to David.*] And thou art David ? Thou art the chief of the beggars ? Shall I strike thee, too, with my staff ? Thou — Is my wife here with you ? I have been told that she went to thee with much food. It was all false — I'll have the informants' tongues cut out. They lied to me. They hatched up a false accusation. Ye are all starving as before . . . As before ye all beg upon the roads . . . Hungry dogs ! . . . Empty stomachs ! . . . But my wife — Where is my wife ? She is not at home . . . I could find her nowhere . . . Was she not here with thee ? Speak, slave, hast thou not seen my wife ? Were I to find her here ! . . . I'd strip her naked here before your very eyes — You never saw my wife naked ? Her body is so sweet to kiss ! Hey ! hey !

ABIGAIL.

[*Behind the stone.*]

Fie !

NABAL.

[*Looking about.*]

Hey ?

[*About to look behind the stone.*]

DAVID.

[*Obstructs his way.*]

NABAL.

Hey, hey ! I'd strip her naked right here and
let her have it upon her bare body with this staff . . .
I shall do it anyway . . . She was not at home . . .
the harlot, the gadabout . . . On her bare body
with staff and thong . . .

DAVID.

[*Seizes Nabal by the throat and commences to
choke him.*]

ASAHEL, ABISHUR AND AHIMELECH.

[*Rush forward and commence to thrust at
Nabal with their swords.*]

ABIGAIL.

[*Rises slowly from behind the stone to see why
Nabal has suddenly become silent. Behold-
ing the struggle, she stifles the outcry which
her terror brings to her lips.*]

DAVID.

[*Throws Nabal away from him.*]

ABIGAIL.

[*Her eyes turned toward Nabal, she sinks
slowly behind the stone.*]

NABAL.

[*Falls on the ground in his entire length, but soon arises, passing his hand over his face and looking quite sober. Finally his gaze lights upon David and he works himself up to a terrible fit of anger, doubling his fists.*]

Thou knowest my wife ! . . . She has been here with thee ! . . . Thou trailer after married women ! Thou low fellow ! Thou slave, which thy master hath not whipped enough ! . . .

ASAHEL, ABISHUR AND AHIMELECH.
[*Rush upon Nabal with drawn swords.*]

DAVID.

Back ! Let not a hair of his head be harmed ! I have sworn it ! . . .

NABAL.

Thou coward ! Night-robber ! Thou runaway slave !

ABIGAIL.

[*Jumping up.*]
Hold ! Enough! Cease thy contumely !

NABAL.

[*With distended eyes.*]
She is here ! . . . She is here with thee ! . . .

ABIGAIL.

[*Steps slowly forth from her hiding place, her eyes lowered.*]

He hath earned thy thanks, and thy blessing, not thy rude words.

NABAL.

[*Completely sober by now.*]

She is here, the —

ABIGAIL.

Neither abuse me. Call me no names. I am here for thy sake. I came hither to save thee from his avenging wrath . . . to save thy possessions and the lives of all of us.

NABAL.

Hast thou brought him thyself as gift ?

DAVID.

[*Makes a threatening gesture.*]

ABIGAIL.

How canst thou speak thus ? Shame thyself, so to address me !

NABAL.

Didst thou come with empty hands and smooth words to appease him ?

ABIGAIL.

I brought him gifts.

NABAL.

Gifts ! Tell me the truth !

ABIGAIL.

Rouse not thyself.   Thine anger is uncalled for.

NABAL.

Gifts ? !

ABIGAIL.

Nothing great.   An insignificant part of that which thou hast.

NABAL.

Gifts ! Tell me ! Which ? What ? How much ?

ABIGAIL.

Two hundred loaves of bread . . .

NABAL.

Ttt-two h-hundred loaves ? . . . Continue . . .

ABIGAIL.

Two bottles of wine . . .

NABAL.

Yes, go on !

ABIGAIL.

Five sheep . . .

NABAL.

Sheep ! . . . Sheep ! . . . What else ? !

ABIGAIL.

Five measures of parched corn . . .

NABAL.

Indeed ! Five of everything . . . Five . . . Five
. . . Five times five most likely !

ABIGAIL.

As true as God liveth . . .

NABAL.

Continue ! Continue ! Give the complete tale !
What more ? How many oxen ? How many
cattle ? How many goats ? And milk ? And
butter ?

ABIGAIL.

Oh, nay ! Oh, nay ! Nothing of all these !
Only an hundred clusters of raisins and two hundred . . .

NABAL.

Ttt-two hundred ? ! . . . What ? ! . . .

ABIGAIL.

Cakes of figs.

NABAL.

Figcakes ! Two hundred figcakes ! Figcakes ! Figcakes ! Two hundred ! Thou ! . . . Thou ! . . .

ABIGAIL.

[*About to shield herself from Nabal behind David.*]

NABAL.

Thou ! . . .

[*His breath comes short, he gasps, his hands at his neck.*]

ASAHEL, ABISHUR, AHIMELECH.

[*Surround Nabal with bread, meat, cakes and wine which they thrust before his eyes.*]

Seest ? Thy bread it is we eat ! . . . Thy cakes . . . Thy figcakes ! Figcakes ! . . .

NABAL.

[*Falls suddenly to the ground.*]

ABIGAIL.

[*With a shriek of fright she approaches Nabal carefully.*]

Nabal ! [*He is motionless, and she bends over him.*] Nabal ! [*She gets down on her knees and looks for signs of life.*] Nabal ! . . . [*Frightened, looking around to David.*] He is dead !

DAVID.

[*Bending over.*]
He is dead. [*As if to himself.*] Blessed be God that hath reckoned with my insult from Nabal, and hath kept me from evil. Nabal's wickedness hath returned upon his own head. [*To Abigail.*] Thou, too, mayst praise the Lord.

ABIGAIL.

He is dead.

DAVID.

And thou art free and delivered from the hand of a wicked man.

ABIGAIL.

God is my witness. I did not wish his death.

DAVID.

Thou pure and faithful soul !

ABIGAIL.

But he called thee such vile names . . .

DAVID.

[*Puts his hand slowly upon her head, and caresses her hair.*]

ABIGAIL.

[*Shudders and closes her eyes. She soon opens them, and looks upon the corpse.*]

I feel shame that I cannot weep ... Yet can I not weep ...

DAVID.

[*To Asahel and his comrades.*]

Take him away. Carry him back to his earth in Carmel and bury him there with his forefathers.

AHIMELECH

To the dogs would I ...

DAVID.

Silence ! ...

ASAHEL.

It is a pity ! Poor dogs ! Such a tough fellow ...
[*They carry out the corpse.*]

ABIGAIL.

[*Arising in tears.*]

Nabal !

DAVID.

Thou hast spoken his name for the last time.

ABIGAIL.

[*Shaking her head.*]

Nay. He was my husband —

DAVID.

Was. But now — I —

ABIGAIL.
[*Raising her eyes to his.*]

Wouldst thou ?

DAVID.

Take his place.

ABIGAIL.

Oh !

DAVID.

Wilt thou be my wife ? If that be true which I
have read from thine eyes . . .

ABIGAIL.
[*Lowers her head, gradually bows low, and
falls of a sudden upon her knees.*]

Thine handmaid will be a servant to wash the
feet of the servants of my lord.

DAVID.
[*Raises her, embracing her.*]

My wife ! My pious dove !

CURTAIN

FORGOTTEN SOULS
Drama in One Act

By DAVID PINSKI

PERSONS

FANNY SEGAL, *owner of a tailoring establishment.*

LIZZIE EHRLICH, *a pianist* ⎫
⎬ *Miss Segal's*
HINDES, *a teacher* ⎭ *Boarders.*

PLACE, *a Russian provincial town.*

TIME, *the present.*

FORGOTTEN SOULS

SCENE: *Workroom at Fanny Segal's. A door to the left of the spectator, another in the back. A large table, covered with various materials; at each side of the table a sewing machine. On the wall to the right, a three-panelled mirror; in the corner, a large wardrobe. Not far from the wardrobe two dressmaker's forms, covered with cloaks. In the middle a broad armchair. Evening.*

FANNY.

[Runs out through the rear door and soon returns with a letter in her hand. She tears it nervously open and is absorbed in reading. Suddenly she gives a scream of delight.]

Oh ! — Oh ! *[Passes her hand over her face and through her hair, looks at the letter, cries out anew, breathing with difficulty. Looks at the letter once more, and exclaims, heavily.]* You ! My love ! My love! *[She is lost for a moment in thought, then calls.]* Lizzie ! Lizzie ! Lizzie !

53

LIZZIE.

[*Enters, dressed up as if for a ball, sticking
a pin in her hat. Mocks Fanny's tone.*]

What's up? What's up? What's up?

FANNY.

Read this! Quickly! It's from Berman!

LIZZIE.

[*Takes the letter.*]

Why see! We've just been talking about him.
And they really accepted his drama?

[*Looks at the letter.*]

FANNY.

[*Looks on, too, in great excitement.*]

LIZZIE.

[*As she reads.*]

That's fine! [*Turns over a page and continues
reading.*] Why! This is an actual proposal of
marriage, Fanny, my dear!

FANNY.

[*Her breath short from delight.*]

Did you understand it that way, too?

LIZZIE.

[*Still looking at the letter.*]
How can it be interpreted otherwise ? [*About to read the letter aloud.*] Ahem ! [*Reads with a certain solemnity.*] "My drama has been accepted and will be produced this very winter. The conditions of the contract are first-rate, and the director promises me a great success, and incidentally a great reputation." [*Reads over some passages in an indistinct nasal monotone, then continues.*] "My ! You ought to see me now. — I've sung and danced so much that it'll be a wonder to me if I'm not asked to move. I feel so strong. And now to write, to create, to do things !" [*Reads again in a nasal monotone, and soon with greater solemnity than before, and a certain tenderness.*] "And now, I hope, better days are in store for us, happiness of such a nature that you cannot be indifferent to it." [*Stops reading.*] That's a bit veiled, but it's plain talk just the same. [*Gives Fanny the letter. Speaks lovingly.*] Lucky woman ! My darling Fanny ! [*Embraces her.*] You dear ! [*Kisses her.*]

FANNY.

So that's the way you understand it, too ? [*Speaks in gasps, trembling all over.*] Oh ! Oh!
[*Covers her face with the letter, takes it to her lips and breathes with difficulty. She takes,*

from her right sleeve, a handkerchief and wipes her eyes.]

LIZZIE.
[*Moved, embracing her with both arms.*]
My dear Fanny ! How happy I am ! You dear, you ! [*Dreamily.*] Now I know how I'll play at the Ginsberg's tonight ! I'll put my whole soul into the music, and it will be the merriest, cheeriest soul that ever lived in the world.

FANNY.
[*Bends down and kisses her forehead.*]
My faithful friend !

LIZZIE.
At last ! My dream's come true !

FANNY.
[*Drops into the armchair.*]
Your dream ?

LIZZIE.
[*Takes a piece of cloth from the table, spreads it out on the floor, and kneels before Fanny.*]
Listen. I dreamed for you a hero before whom the world, even before seeing him, would bare its head. I dreamed for you a triumphal march of powerful harmonies, a genius, a superman, such as only you deserve.

FANNY.
Sh! Sh! Don't talk like that!

LIZZIE.
No, no. You can't take that away from me. As long as I shall live I'll never cease admiring you. There aren't many sisters in the world like you. Why, you never have given a thought to yourself, never a look, but have worked with might and main to make a somebody out of your sister. I'll tell you the truth. I've often had the most unfriendly feelings toward your sister Olga. She takes it so easy there in Petrograd, while you —

FANNY.
[*Tenderly.*]

You're a naughty girl.

LIZZIE.
I simply couldn't see how things went on, — how you were working yourself to death.

FANNY.
But that was my happiness, and now I am amply repaid for it, to see Olga placed upon an independent footing, with a great future before her as a painter.

LIZZIE.
That kind of happiness did not appeal very much to me. I wanted, for you, a different kind

of happiness, — the happiness of being a wife, of being a mother, of loving and being loved.

FANNY.

[*In a reverie.*]

I had already weaned my thoughts away from love and family life as the only happiness.

LIZZIE.

You poor soul !

FANNY.

When my mother died, my road was clearly mapped out for me: to be to my sister, who is eight years younger than I, both a father and a mother. That purpose was great and holy to me. I never thought of anything else. Only in the early twenties, between twenty-two and twenty-five, a longing for something else came to me. Not that my sister became a burden to me, God forbid, but I wanted something more, a full life, happiness and — love. At that time I used to cry very much, and wet my pillow with my tears, and I was very unhappy. And I was easily angered then, too, so you see I was far from an angel.

LIZZIE.

[*Draws Fanny nearer, and kisses her.*]

You darling, you !

FANNY.

But later the longing left me, as if it had been charmed away. Olga grew older, and her talents began to ripen. Then I forgot myself altogether, and she became again my sole concern.

LIZZIE.

And is that all ?

FANNY.

What else can there be ? Of course, when my sister went to Petrograd she was no longer under my immediate care and I was left all alone. The old longing re-awoke in my bosom but I told myself that one of my years had no right to expect happiness and love. So I determined to tear out, to uproot from my heart every longing. I tried to convince myself that my goal in life had already been attained — that I had placed a helpless child securely upon her feet —

LIZZIE.

But you loved Berman all the time, didn't you ?

FANNY.

Yes, I loved him all the time, but I fought my feelings. Life had taught me to restrain and to suppress my desires. I argued: He is too far above me —

LIZZIE.

Too far above you ?

FANNY.

[*Continuing.*]

And I am too worn-out for him. And further-more, I tried to make myself believe that his daily visits here were accidental, that they were not intended for me at all, but for his friend and nephew Hindes, who happens to board with me.

LIZZIE.

But how could you help perceiving that he was something more than indifferent to you ? You must have been able to read it in his eyes.

FANNY.

[*Smiling.*]

Well, you see how it is ! And perhaps for the very reason that I had abandoned all ideas of love, and had sought to deceive myself into believing that I was a dried-up twig on the tree of life —

LIZZIE.

[*Jumping up.*]

My ! How you sinned against yourself !

FANNY.

[*Rising.*]

But now the sap and the strength flow again within me, — now I am young once more. — Ah ! Life, life ! — To enjoy it, to drink it down in copious draughts, to feel it in every pulse-beat — Oh, Lizzie, play me a triumphal march, a song of joy, of jubilation . . .

LIZZIE.

So that the very walls will dance and the heavens join in the chorus. [*Goes to the door at the left, singing.*] "Joy, thou goddess, fair, immortal, daughter of Elysium, Mad with rapture —" [*Suddenly stops.*] Sh ! Hindes is coming !

[*Listens.*]

FANNY.

[*She has been standing as if entranced; her whole body trembles as she awakens to her surroundings. She puts her finger to her nose, warningly.*]

Don't say a word to him about it.

LIZZIE.

I will ! He must know it, he must be happy over it, too. And if he truly loves you, he will be happy to learn it. And then, once for all he'll get rid of his notions about winning you.

FANNY.

Don't be so inconsiderate.

LIZZIE.

Leave it to me ! . . . Hindes ! Hindes !

FANNY.

It's high time you left for the Ginsberg's.

LIZZIE.

I've a few minutes yet . . . Hindes ! Hindes !

HINDES.

[*Appears at the rear door. He wears spectacles; under his left arm a crutch, under his right arm books, and in his hands various bags of food.*]

FANNY.

[*Steals out through the door at the left.*]

HINDES.

Good evening. What's the news ?

LIZZIE.

Come here ! Quick ! Fa —

HINDES.

Won't you give me time to carry my parcels into my room ?

LIZZIE.

Not even a second ! Fanny has —

HINDES.

[*Taking an apple from a bag.*]

Have an apple.

LIZZIE.

[*Refusing it.*]

Let me speak, won't you ! Fa —

HINDES.

May I at least sit down ?

LIZZIE.

[*Loudly.*]

Fanny has received a letter from Berman !

HINDES.

[*Taking a seat.*]

Saying that his drama has been accepted. I, too, have received a letter from Berman.

LIZZIE.

That's nothing. The point is that he is seeking to make a match with her. He has practically proposed to her.

HINDES.

[*Astonished.*]

Practically proposed ? To Fanny ?

LIZZIE.

Yes, and when Fanny comes back you just see
to it that you wish her a right friendly congrat-
ulation, and that you make no — [*Stops suddenly.*]
Hm ! I came near saying something silly. — Oh,
I'm so happy, and I'd just have the whole world
happy with me. Do you hear ? You must help
her celebrate, do you hear ? And now, good night
to you, for I must run along to the Ginsberg's.
[*Turns to the door at the left singing.* "Joy, thou
goddess, fair, immortal . . . "

HINDES.

[*Calling after her.*]

But — the devil. Miss Ehrlich !

LIZZIE.

[*At the door.*]

I haven't a single moment to spare for the devil.
[*She disappears.*]

HINDES.

[*Grunts angrily, throws his crutch to the
ground, places his books and his packages
on a chair, and mumbles.*]

What mockery is this !
> [*Takes out a letter from his inside pocket
> and reads it over several times. Grunts
> again. Rests his head heavily upon his
> hand, and looks vacantly forward, as if
> deeply puzzled.*]

FANNY.
> [*Enters, embarrassed.*]

Good evening, Hindes !

HINDES.
> [*Mumbles, without changing his position.*]

Good evening !

FANNY.
> [*Looks at him in embarrassment, and begins
> to busy herself with the cloaks on the forms.*]

HINDES.
> [*Still in the same position. He taps his foot
> nervously. He soon ceases this, and speaks
> without looking at Fanny.*]

Miss Segal, will you permit me to see Berman's
letter ?

FANNY.
> [*With a nervous laugh.*]

That's a bit indiscreet — not at all like a cav-
alier.

HINDES.

[*Same position and same tone.*]

Will you permit me to see Berman's letter?

FANNY.

[*With a laugh of embarrassment, throws him the letter, which she has been holding in her sleeve.*]

Read it, if that's how you feel.

HINDES.

[*Bends slowly down, gets the letter, commences to read it, and then to grumble.*]

Hm! So!

[*He lets the letter fall to his knee, and stares vacantly before him. He shakes his foot nervously and mumbles as if to himself.*]

To be such an idiot!

FANNY.

[*Regards him with astonishment.*]

HINDES.

[*Somewhat more softly.*]

To be such an idiot!

FANNY.

[*Laughing, still embarrassed.*]

Who?

HINDES.

Not I.

> [*Picks up his crutch, the books and the parcels,
> arises, and gives the letter to Fanny.*]

FANNY.

> [*Beseechingly.*]

Hindes, don't take it so badly.   You make me
very sad.

HINDES.

I'm going to my room, so you won't see me.

FANNY.

> [*As before.*]

Don't speak to me like that, Hindes.   Be my
good friend, as you always were.   [*In a lower tone,
embarrassed.*]   And be good to Berman.   For you
know, between us, between you and me, there
could never have been anything more than friendship.

HINDES.

There is no need of your telling me that.   I
know what I know and have no fault to find with
you.

FANNY.

Then why are you so upset, and why do you
reproach yourself ?

HINDES.

Because . . .

FANNY.

Because what ?

HINDES.
[*After an inner struggle, stormily.*]
Because I am in a rage ! To think of a chap writing such a veiled, ambiguous, absolutely botched sentence, and cooking up such a mess !

FANNY.
What do you mean by all this ?

HINDES.
You know, Miss Segal, what my feelings are toward you, and you know that I wish you all happiness. I assure you that I would bury deep within me all my grief and all my longing, and would rejoice with a full heart — if things were as you understood them from Berman's letter.

FANNY.
As I understood them from Berman's letter ?

HINDES.
— And what rouses my anger and makes me hesitate is that it should have had to happen to

you and that I must be the surgeon to cut the
cataract from your eye.

FANNY.

[*Astounded.*]

Drop your rhetorical figures.   End your work.
Cut away, since you've begun the cutting.

HINDES.

[*Without looking at her, deeply stirred.*]
Berman did not mean you.

FANNY.

Not me ?

HINDES.

Not you, but your sister.

FANNY.

[*With an outcry.*]

Oh ! —

HINDES.

He writes me that his first meeting with her was
as if the splendor of God had suddenly shone down
upon him, — that gradually he was inflamed by a
fiery passion, and that he hopes his love is returned,
that . . .

FANNY.

[*Falls upon a chair, her face turned toward the table. She breaks into moaning.*]

She has taken from me everything !

[*In deepest despair, with cries from her innermost being, she tears at her hair.*]

HINDES.

[*Drops his books and packages to the floor. Limps over to Fanny, and removes her hands from her head.*]

You have good reason to weep, but not to harm yourself.

FANNY.

[*Hysterically.*]

She has taken from me everything ! My ambition to study, my youth, my fondest hopes, and now . . .

HINDES

And now ? — Nothing. As you see, Berman never loved you. If it hadn't been for that unfortunate, ambiguous, absolutely botched, simply idiotic sentence . . .

FANNY

[*Softly.*]

Hindes, I feel that I no longer care to live.

HINDES.
Folly !

FANNY.
I feel as if my heart had been torn in two. My soul is empty, desolate . . . as if an abyss had opened before me . . . What have I now to live for ? I can live no longer !

HINDES.
Folly ! Nonsense !

FANNY.
I have already lived my life . . .

HINDES.
Absurd !

FANNY.
[*Resolutely.*]
I know what I'm talking about, and I know what to do.

[*Silence.*]

HINDES.
[*Regarding her closely. With blunt emphasis.*]
You're thinking now over what death you shall choose.

FANNY.
[*Motionless.*]

HINDES.

[Taking a seat.]

Let me tell you a story. There was once upon a time a man who — not through doubt and misfortune, but rather through good times and pleasures came to the conclusion that life wasn't worth living. So he went off to buy a revolver. On his way a great clamor arose in the street. A house had caught fire and in a moment was in flames. Suddenly, at one of the windows in the top story there appeared a woman. The firemen had placed their highest ladders against the building and a man began to climb up. That man was none other than our candidate for suicide. He took the woman out of the window, gave her to the firemen who had followed him up, and then went through the window into the house. The surrounding crowd trembled with fear lest the house should cave in at the very next moment. Flames already appeared at the window, and people were sure that the hero had been burned to death inside. But he had not been burned; he soon appeared on the roof, with a small child in his arms. The ladders could not reach to this height, so the firemen threw him a rope. He tied the rope about the child and lowered it to the firemen. But he himself was beyond rescue. He folded his hands over his heart, and tears trickled from his eyes. He, who but a moment before had sought death, now desired not to die. No, he wanted to live, for in that moment he had found a purpose: to live and to do good.

FANNY.

[*Angrily*.]

To do good ! I'm tired of doing good !

HINDES.

Don't sin against yourself, Fanny !

FANNY.

Do good ! I have done good; I have lived for others, not myself; and now you can see for yourself that I have not fulfilled my life. I feel as wretched as the most miserable, as the most wicked, and I long for death even as the most unhappy !

HINDES.

[*Looking at her from under his spectacles*.]
Does Olga know of your feelings toward Berman ?

FANNY.

[*Angrily*.]

I don't know what she knows.

HINDES.

Can't you give me any better reply than that ?

FANNY.

What can I know ? I used to write her letters just full of Berman.

HINDES.

Could Olga have gathered from them that you were not indifferently disposed toward him ?

FANNY.

What do you mean by this cross-examination ?

HINDES.

I have a notion that if you were to do what you have in your mind at present, — a thing I cannot bring myself to name, — then Olga would not accept Berman's love. Rather she would take her own life, since she would look upon herself as the cause of your death.

FANNY.

What's this you've thought up ?

HINDES.

Just what you heard.

FANNY.

And you mean — ?

HINDES.

— That you know your sister and ought to realize what she's liable to do.

FANNY.

[In a fit of anger.]

First she takes away my life, and now she will not let me die ! *[Her head sinks to the table.]*

HINDES.

There spoke the true Fanny, the Fanny of yore.

FANNY.

[Weeps bitterly.]

HINDES.

Well may you weep. Weep, Fanny, weep until the tears come no more. But when that is over, then dry your eyes and never weep again. Dry forever the source of all your tears. That's exactly what I did, do you understand ? Such people as you and I, robbed of personal happiness, must either weep forever, or never weep at all. I chose the latter course. Harden yourself, Fanny, and then fold your arms on your breast and look fearlessly forward into life, fulfilling it as your heart dictates.

FANNY.

[Continues weeping.]

HINDES.

[*Noticing Berman's letter on the table, takes it up and throws it down angrily.*]

Such a botched, idiotic sentence! And he's a poet!

FANNY.

[*Raising her head.*]

If things are as you say, then Olga will in any case reject Berman. She will imagine that she is taking him away from me, and such a thing she would never do.

HINDES.

Perhaps. [*Suddenly, bluntly.*] And what will be the effect of all this upon you ?

FANNY.

[*Brokenly.*]

Who's thinking of self ? I mean that I want her to have him.

HINDES.

There's the old Fanny again !

FANNY.

Ah ! Enough of that ! Better help me with some suggestion.

HINDES.

Some suggestion ? Be her matchmaker.

FANNY.

And suppose she should turn the tables and want to be my matchmaker ?

HINDES.

We've got to think that over.

[*Silence.*]

FANNY.

[*Brokenly.*]

Hindes !

HINDES.

What ?

FANNY.

I have an idea.

HINDES.

Good.

FANNY.

But I need your aid.

HINDES.

Count on me, if I'm able.

FANNY.

Do you promise ?

HINDES.

Blindly ?

FANNY.

Blindly.

HINDES.

[*Looks at her.*]
Why must I promise you blindly ? If I'm able,
you may be sure I'll help.

FANNY.

[*Brokenly, yet in embarrassment.*]
Take me . . . Marry me.

HINDES.

[*For a moment he looks at her, then picks up
his crutch, his books and the packages.*]

FANNY.

[*Beseechingly.*]
Hindes ! If I should marry, Olga wouldn't have
any obstacle in her way.

HINDES.

Miss Segal, I have loved you, and still do.   But
I refuse to be the altar upon which you shall sacrifice yourself.

FANNY.

But a moment ago you dissuaded me from death.
Will you now drive me back to it ?

HINDES.

Your sister will be able to find happiness without
Berman.

FANNY.

But if she loves him ? —

HINDES.

Then she'll suffer, just as we do.

FANNY.

No ! Olga must not suffer ! Do you hear !
I'll not have it !

HINDES.

That is very nice of you.

FANNY.

[*Through her tears.*]

Hindes, I no longer know you.

HINDES.

[*Turns toward the door.*]

Good night.

FANNY.
[*Is overcome by sobbing.*]

HINDES.
[*Limps to the door, then stops. Looks down-
wards, then raises his eyes toward Fanny.*]
Miss Segal, why is it that during all the time
that I have boarded with you I have made no
declaration of love, that I have never proposed
marriage ?

FANNY.
[*Weeps.*]

HINDES.
I'll tell you. Wasn't it because I knew that you
didn't love me, and because I wanted your love,
not merely your respect ?

FANNY.
[*Firmly.*]
No. You didn't do it simply because you knew
that I would refuse you.

HINDES.
And suppose I expected "Yes" from you ?

FANNY.
Then you would have proposed.

HINDES.

And married you without your love ?

FANNY.

Yes.

HINDES.

But then I didn't know that you loved another.

FANNY.

[*Brokenly.*]

The other no longer exists for me.

HINDES.

[*Looks again at the floor.   Silence.*]

FANNY.

Hindes !

HINDES.

Yes ?

FANNY.

Come nearer to me.

HINDES.

I am lame.

FANNY.

Put all your bundles aside.

HINDES.

[*Hesitates for a moment, then puts down his
books and packages.*]

FANNY.
[*As if in embarrassment.*]
Everything . . . Everything . . .

HINDES.
[*Bluntly*]
Don't be ashamed. Say just what you mean:
Lay aside the crutch, too.
[*He lays aside the crutch.*]

FANNY.
[*Arises, takes his hand.*]
Hindes, you know my attitude toward you.
You know how highly I esteem you, how happy I've
always been to possess in you a good, true friend . . .
[*Nestles her head against him, coyly.*] Embrace me,
and give me a kiss, a hot, passionate kiss. Put
into it your whole love, make it express your whole
true soul. [*Brokenly, and in tears.*] I tell you,
our life will be — happy. We souls, forgotten by
happiness, will yet find it — in our own way — as
best we can. [*Less tearfully.*] You'll see how it'll
soon be. Lizzie will come home and she'll play us a
march of jubilation, a march of joy . . . [*Brokenly.*]
She owes it to me ! . . . I'll dance, I tell you; I'll

dance for two. You'll see. And I'll sing. I'll turn things upside down. Hindes, kiss me, hotly, hotly.

HINDES.
[*Passionately, through tears.*]
You . . . You . . .
[*He gives her a long kiss, as if entranced.*]

SLOW CURTAIN

SOLOMON J. RABINOWITSCH

Sholom Aleichem is the most popular of some half-dozen pseudonyms that have served to obscure the real name of the author, — Solomon J. Rabinowitsch, (died May 13, 1916). *Sholom Aleichem* is Hebrew for "Peace be with you" and is a common greeting when two Jews meet. It was a happy thought of the author's to choose as his pseudonym a phrase that is so frequently upon Jewish lips, and by the full-blooded humor that has come to be associated with his name he achieved the distinction of being the most beloved of modern Jewish writers. Sholom Aleichem was also known as the Yiddish Mark Twain.

Rabinowitsch was born about fifty-seven years ago in Poltova, Russia. He is a figure of far greater importance to Yiddish letters than to the Yiddish stage, and was responsible for the revival of Yiddish poetry some thirty years ago. He gave a new trend to his people's literature, as editor established new standards, and as critic demolished the vulgar type of work for which Shaikewitsch's name has long stood as symbol. Sholom Aleichem learned his style from the Russians Gogol and Ostrovsky, whom he much resembles in his humorous writings. As poet he seems to have been nurtured upon Nekrassof.

He is not primarily a dramatist. The play here presented, entitled in the original *A Doktor!* is given for its comic treatment of the matchmaker theme, and as an example of Yiddish vaudeville, rather for any dramaturgic or intellectual merit. It illustrates, at the same time, that spirit of amusement for amusement's sake which is characteristic of the writer's prose works, not without its undercurrent of thought or satire. The Jew can rarely laugh without thinking, and, quite as important, is always ready to laugh at himself.

It is only fair to say that Rabinowitsch did not profess to be a great dramatist. Other one-act efforts, as for instance *"Mazel Tov"* [Good luck, i. e. Congratulations] and *Der Get* [The Divorce] show clearly his limitations. Either the pathos becomes bathos, or the comedy degenerates to vaudeville. His *"Zeseit und Zerspreit"* [Cast to the Winds, literally, Disseminated and Dispersed] in three acts, had some success in Poland, and bears a strong resemblance to Naidenof's "Children of Vaniouschin". It is the tale of a family's disintegration.

A Doktor! cannot, of course, be appreciated as much by the Gentile as by the Jew, to whom the marriage-broker type is, today, a more or less comical, if at times necessary, personage.

Although we have no less an authority than the *Talmud* for the statements that "marriages are made in heaven", and that "not money but character is the best dowry of a wife," the professional matchmaker or marriage-broker [shadchan] is still an important factor in modern Yiddish life. True, he has fallen from the position of legal and social pre-eminence which he enjoyed some centuries ago, yet today he does a flourishing business in defiance of both Talmudic citations. "After all," he might argue, "I make marriages on earth, but then, is it not possible that in so doing I am an intermediary of heaven?" To which, no doubt, many a Jewish maiden will assent who, favored much more by fortune than by Nature, would otherwise be condemned to remain in that state which to her is far more certainly a singleness than a blessedness. And as for character being the best dowry, no parent ever told that to a shadchan; some poor father of homely daughters must have smuggled that line into the Talmud. However that may be, characters yield no percentage, and the shadchan, before singing the epithalamium consults, if you will, the Yiddish Bradstreet and Dun.

"The professional matchmaker", says a well-known authority, "comes into prominence and enjoys a legal status at least as early as the twelfth century. It is hardly open to doubt that this enterprising professional owed his existence to the same cycle of events which resulted in the systematization of early marriages. When Jewish society became disintegrated by the massacres and expulsions of the crusading era, its scattered items could only be re-united through the agency of some peripatetic go-between. There was nothing essentially unromantic about the method, for the *schadchan* was often a genuine enthusiast for marriage. The evil came in when, like the Roman *proxuba* or the Moslem *katbeh*, the *schadchan* made up marriages for a fee, or, happening to be a traveling merchant, hawked hearts as well as trinkets.''

In early times none but a student of the holy law might be a matchmaker. One famous Rabbi devoted the whole of his income as Rabbi to the support of his students, maintaining himself by his matchmaker fees. In the middle ages, when parents were anxious to marry their daughters to men of learning the Rabbi was a natural go-between.

The matchmaker's fee was usually a percentage of the dowry. Thus, "in the middle of the eighteenth century the *shadchan* in the Black Forest received one and one-half per cent on dowries of 600 gulden, and one per cent on dowries of larger amount." In earlier times the sum might be made the matter of special bargaining, and thus represent more than the regular rates. A rare case is cited of a Jewish female matchmaker (*shadchanis*) with the added rarity that she declared her girl client four years *older* than she really was! All of which becomes more easily understandable when we are told that the girl was twelve.

The term shadchan is derived, most appropriately, from a Hebrew word signifying, literally, *the charmer*. In modern literature and on the Yiddish stage the shadchan's charming talk usually takes the form of downright lying. In actual life, although the conditions of the ghetto still allow of his activity, he is slowly but certainly being ousted by the determination of the young folks to be their own matchmakers. The modern Jewish girl is feminist enough to see the degrading commercialism inherent in the *shadchan's* trade and to recognize the insult to her individualism which is thus implied. At the same time this type is not yet so numerous but that, in the chase after doctors and lawyers which distinguishes many who should be above the purchase of husbands, the shadchan still finds employment.

SHE MUST MARRY A DOCTOR

DOCTOR

Sketch in One Act

By SOLOMON J. RABINOWITSCH

(SHOLOM ALEICHEM)

PERSONS

HYMAN KRENDELMAN, *about 50 years of age, — just become rich. Wears a long coat, but no hat.*

ANNA, *his wife, of uncertain age . . . Manages to keep young by mixing with the up-to-date youngsters. Lavishly bedecked with ornaments of gold, diamonds, brilliants and pearls.*

VERA, *their daughter,— a young, modernized girl.*

ABRAM, *their son, of the studious, modern sort.*

SHOLOM THE MATCHMAKER,— *in a green coat and a skull-cap.*

SLOTTKE, *a chambermaid.*

BREINE, *the cook,— a woman with a hairy upper-lip.*

SHE MUST MARRY A DOCTOR

SCENE: *A large parlor, containing costly velvet-upholstered furniture, expensive rugs, bronze-framed mirrors, various tables. There is a display of silver plates, gilded spoons, colored glasses. The arm-chairs are strewn with silk and satin dresses. On the window a large copper pot with two handles. Costly, but dried-up plants, on which are hanging a pair of brushed pants and a white vest. On a book-shelf may be seen bread-crumbs and a jar of preserves. On the piano, a pillow. In short — a picture of rare disorder.*

HYMAN.
[*Gesticulating wildly and running about the room.*]

Good God in heaven, what is he pestering the life out of me for ?

SHOLOM.
[*Running after him, with a letter in his hand.*]

Here, see, read for yourself what they write me. Read ! Do you think I want to fool you, eh ?

HYMAN.

But I tell you I want none of this ! I don't want any match ! That's all there is to it ! What on earth are you pestering me about ?

SHOLOM.

But I ask nothing of you,— nothing at all, except that you shall have the kindness to take the trouble and read this letter here that I've received.

HYMAN.

What have you against me, anyway ? For heaven's sake, leave me in peace, will you ? I have no time to talk with you. Come some other day, won't you ? What on earth is he pestering me for !

SHOLOM.

[*To himself.*]

It doesn't become him to listen. He's on his high horse . . . He doesn't want to give a dowry, that's the trouble, — the miser ! [*To Hyman.*] May you live to be a hundred and twenty years old ! Just take a glance at a few lines, just a couple of words, my dear fellow. Why should you care ? Just do it as a favor to me, that's all. Believe me, I tell you by my faith, I tell you, it's one cracker-jack proposition, — Such an opportunity doesn't

come once in ten years. Here, take the letter,
read it with your own eyes, — here, read.

HYMAN.
[*Stopping both his ears.*]
Good heavens ! What misfortune is this ?
What visitation of wrath has been sent upon me ?
Stop pestering me, I tell you ! It's positively
unbearable ! My, oh my, oh my !
[*His wife comes running in.*]

ANNA.
[*Frightened.*]
What's the trouble ?

HYMAN.
[*About to speak, but Sholom prevents him by
stopping his mouth. With his other hand
Sholom waves about the letter.*]
Mm — mm —

SHOLOM.
Understand me, my dear Mrs. Krendelman,
may you ever be well and happy, — I'll show you
the letter. Why should we deceive ourselves ?
Why ? I tell you it's a rare good fortune for your
daughter. Upon my very life I swear it ! Here,
take it, read, — read and see for yourself that I'm
telling no fibs. Why should I lead you into any

affair that you'll regret — God forbid ! Here, see
for yourself, — here, read, — here ! . . .

ANNA.

*[Takes the letter and puts it into her husband's
hand.]*

Really, Hyman, why shouldn't you read it ?
What harm can it do you ? Does it cost you any
money ?

HYMAN.

*[Takes the letter. Puts on a pair of silver
spectacles, sits down and commences to
read in a very loud voice. Anna sits down
nearby, while Sholom accompanies the reading with a nodding of the head and smacking
of the lips after each phrase. He fairly
glows with satisfaction.]*

"To the honorable, beloved, worthy, esteemed,
learned, wealthy, pious Mr. Sholom the Matchmaker, may his light shine forever: In the first
place, let me say, that I am well, — praised be
God, — and hope to hear the same from you, —
may the future bring nothing worse — Amen.
In the second place, in regard to the daughter of
the wealthy man of whom you wrote me, I'm afraid
that there can be no match arranged with the son
of the rich man over here. Because, in the first
place, you've probably heard of what befell the

rich man over here, — his elder daughter . . . "
What's all this to do with me ? What do I need to
know all this stuff for ?

SHOLOM.
[*Seizing Hyman by the arm.*]
What do you care ? Just keep on reading and
you'll come to the important part.

HYMAN.
[*Continues reading.*]
" . . . His elder daughter, God forbid, became
infatuated with a teacher, and eloped with him
to a certain town, where she wanted to get married
then and there. So the teacher came with his
sweetheart to a rabbi, prepared for the ceremony.
Well, the way it looks, the rabbi didn't want to
perform the marriage, so they went off to the
government rabbi to get married. So the government rabbi said to them, says he . . . " For the
love of heaven, I ask you, what has that to do with
us ? . . .

SHOLOM.
What do you care ? Just read on . . . read on . . .

HYMAN.
[*Red with anger, continues reading.*]
" . . . So the government rabbi said to them,

says he, — 'What do you wish?' says he. So
the teacher says, 'I want you to marry us'. So the
government rabbi says, 'What do you mean, marry
you? Do I know you?' So the teacher says
[*Becoming confused.*] So the government rabbi
says . . . So he says . . . " To the devil with the
whole business! Did you ever hear the like?
[*Mocking.*] "So he said", "so the government
rabbi said," "so then he said." What's all this
say-so to me? What do you want of me, anyway?

> [*He flings the letter away and is about to leave
> the room, when Sholom seizes his hand and
> stops him. Sholom then proceeds to read
> the letter where Hyman left off.*]

SHOLOM.

[*With frequent pauses for a long breath.*]
". . . Ah! There's modern teachers for you . . .
modern doctors . . . So you see, that the rich man
over here is no kind of relative for a man like your
wealthy man to have. But, for that matter, I
have a match to propose for the daughter of your
wealthy client which is in every way better, finer,
more respectable and of better pedigree than the
other. In the town of Lifovetz there is a very
nice widow named Bayle Goldspinder, and although
she isn't as wealthy as your client, she comes of
a very high pedigree, — from Reb Pincus of
Lifovetz. And, more to the point, she has an

only son, a gem of a young man whose like cannot
be discovered in all the lands of the earth, —
handsome, upright, highly educated and possessed
of all virtues. A man, I tell you, who has studied
all the languages, a regular doctor of philosophy,
and even more, against whom all the other doctors
can't hold a candle." * [*To Anna.*] There!
What do you say to a match like that ! You, —
how do they say ? — are a woman of understanding, who knows her business . . .

ANNA.
[*Turning up her nose.*]
No . . . that's not the kind of match we're
looking for.

HYMAN.
We aren't looking for that kind of match.

SHOLOM.
[*Aside.*]
There you are ! You can't touch these newly
rich swells ! The very dome of heaven isn't good
enough for them ! [*To Hyman and Anna.*]   What
kind of match did you want, then ?

ANNA.
We wanted something . . . something . . . in the
nature of a . . . brilliant match !

*Original: "He sticks all the other doctors in his belt."

HYMAN.

Yes sir   A brilliant match !

SHOLOM.

What ? Do you think you're going to make a brilliant catch with your dowry of ten thousand ?

ANNA.

Ten thousand ? You mean twenty thousand !

HYMAN.

Twenty thousand ? No ! I say ten thousand !

SHOLOM.

[*Aside.*]

A fine chance to reach any conclusions here ! Ten thousand, twenty thousand, — twenty thousand, ten thousand. A see-saw between one and the other !

ANNA.

[*Loudly.*]

If I tell you it's twenty thousand, then twenty thousand it is !

SHOLOM.

Twenty thousand, as you say.

HYMAN.

[*Loudly.*]

And when I tell you it's ten thousand, then it's ten, and that's all there is about it !

SHOLOM.

Ten thousand, as you say.

ANNA.

[*Louder.*]

Twenty thousand !

SHOLOM.

Twenty thousand.

HYMAN.

[*Louder.*]

Ten thousand !

SHOLOM.

Ten thousand. [*Aside.*] It's enough to send a man to the lunatic asylum !

[*Abram enters, with a pile of books under his arm. He goes to the bookshelf.*]

HYMAN.

And where are you coming from, pray ?

ABRAM.

[*Looking at nobody.*]

I ? I am coming from the library . . . My ! How hot it is ! [*Notices Sholom.*] Oh ! So Mr. Matchmaker is here again, is he ? What are you doing here, anyway ? Another match ? More bargaining ? When will you learn to deal with up-to-date people ? When are you going to stop buying and selling brides and bridegrooms ? You're worse than Asiatics, savages, despots !

HYMAN.

[*Looks at the matchmaker with pride at Abram's display of learning.*]

There ! What have you to say to that ?

SHOLOM.

[*To Abram.*]

What was that last word you said ?

ABRAM.

And even if I tell you, will you know ?

ANNA.

Why not ? Is Sholom an animal, that he shouldn't understand ?

ABRAM.

Who said he was ? I merely said he wouldn't comprehend, because it is of foreign derivation.

SHOLOM.

Because it's of fo . . . ?

ABRAM.

> [*Close to Sholom's ear.*]

Of foreign derivation.   Now, do you understand?
A word of foreign derivation.

SHOLOM.

Aha !

> [*Abram's parents swell with pride at their
> son's erudition.*]

ABRAM.

Aha ? What do you mean, "aha" ? Right away
the fellow answers, "aha" !

SHOLOM.

I mean, that . . . in regard to the meaning of
that word . . . er, er . . .

> [*Fidgets about with his fingers.*]

ABRAM.

> [*Holding his sides.*]

Ha-ha-ha ! Fanatic ! Oh, you fanatic ! Words
of foreign derivation, you must understand, are
what we would term, in common speech, words
from other languages.   For instance, "despot" is
a word of foreign derivation.   "Despot — despots"
singular, plural.   There ! Do you know where
that word comes from ?

SHOLOM.

Well, where does it come from, pray? I'm
nothing but a common, everyday Jew. I never
went to school, and certainly not through college. . .
Let's have a cigarette, won't you?

[*Abram gives him a cigarette.*]

ABRAM.

[*Pompously.*]

The word despot is derived from "despotism"
. . . Now, do you know?

SHOLOM.

[*Shakes his head.*]

So! . . . And what does despotism mean?

ABRAM.

Despotism is the same as despot.

SHOLOM.

Aha! If that's the case, then I know! Maybe
you have a match about you? [*Abram gives him
a match.*] Now what does despot mean? [*Lights
the cigarette.*] Make that clear for me, won't you?

ABRAM.

Why, a despot is a person who acts despotically.
— There you have the whole story.

SHOLOM.

I understand ! I understand ! [*Blows the smoke of his cigarette into the air.*] And what does despotically mean ?

ABRAM.

Despotically signifies that he acts like a despot. And a despot means a tyrant — despot and tyrant are practically the same, and for heaven's sake don't bother me any longer !
> [*Turns to his books and begins to thumb over the pages.*]

SHOLOM.

I get it now. I get it. The root of the word is one thing, and the meaning of it is another. That's what you call grammar. Tell me, Abram, — long life to you, — from what language does that word come ? From German, or from French ?

ABRAM.
> [*Referring to a book.*]

What ? Despotism ? From Latin.

SHOLOM.
> [*Deeply impressed.*]

You don't say ? All the way from Latin ! [*To Abram's parents.*] You see that ? There's what you call knowing languages ! That's what you call modern learning ! In our day, Hyman, what did we know of tongues and languages ? Eh ?

[*The parents are filled with pride.*]

ABRAM.

[*Haughtily.*]

Who is this proposed husband for my sister that you're talking about ? A doctor of medicine, or a jurist ? Or perhaps a technical engineer ?

SHOLOM.

[*Smoking.*]

Neither one nor the other. —

ABRAM.

Neither one nor the other ? What then is he ? A merchant ?

SHOLOM.

Heaven forbid ! He is a young man of most excellent pedigree, — a man of great learning. Knows every language, — Yiddish, Russian, German, French, and everything else. A regular cyclopedia !

ABRAM.

And you're the connoisseur to judge of his learning, are you ? A fine state of affairs ! But

your trouble is in vain.   My sister will marry no
other than a doctor, and a doctor of medicine,
at that !

HYMAN.

Who's asking you about it, anyway, Abram ?
Who are you to be giving orders around here ?

ABRAM.

Well, I tell you.   Vera will have nobody for a
husband other than a doctor of medicine.

HYMAN.

That may be.   But your business is with your
books, and don't come mixing in to other affairs.
Stick to your books, and the best of health to you !

ANNA.

[*Interrupting.*]

What do you care if our son has his say ?

HYMAN.

I don't like a busy-body.   It's none of his
affair. *

ABRAM.

[*For a while he remains standing, and then
assumes an imposing attitude.   Shakes his
head and speaks to   himself.*]

* Original: "It's no worry of his grandmother's."

Ah ! Despotism ! Fanaticism ! Chassidism, *
Obscurantism !

> [*Exit. Parents drink in each word with
> pride.*]

SHOLOM.

That's a learned fellow for you ! That's what
you call knowledge ! . . . Now then, just where
are we at in regard to the match ? I don't remember, with all this display of learning dinning my
ears . . . Oh, yes . . . Shall I send a telegram or
write a post-card to my partner about the match,
saying that . . .

ANNA.

[*Interrupting.*]

Don't inconvenience yourself. Send no tele-
grams and write no post-cards. The match is
not to our taste.

HYMAN.

No, the match is not to our taste.

SHOLOM.

And why not ?

ANNA.

Because we want a doctor. Now, do you know ?
Once and for all time, she must marry a doctor !
That's what we want for her.

* From Chassid: Member of a fanatical Jewish sect.

SHOLOM.

A doctor, you say ? Well, that's your affair.
If you say doctor, let it be a doctor, then.

HYMAN.

[*To Anna*.]

Doctor, you say ? And you won't have any
other ?

ANNA.

I won't think of any other.

HYMAN.

Well, I'll have you understand that I want a
business man. I've told you time and again that
I want a business man and not a doctor ! A great
bargain you buy with these doctor-poctors. They
study and study, and what does it all amount to ?
When trouble comes, who has to go to whom ?
Who goes borrowing money, I to them, or they to
me ? Say yourself, Mr. Matchmaker. I take
no doctor as son-in-law. My daughter must
marry a business man. You just write that down,
Sholom, — a business man !

SHOLOM.

A business man ? Well, that's your affair. Let
it be business man, since you say so.

ANNA.

Well, just because he says a business man I say it shall be a doctor !

SHOLOM.

A doctor, then.

HYMAN.

[*Loudly.*]

I tell you, Sholom, a business man !

SHOLOM.

All right, a business man.

ANNA.

[*Loudly.*]

I tell you, a doctor !

SHOLOM.

Very well, — a doctor.

HYMAN.

[*Louder.*]

A business man, I say !

SHOLOM.

All right, a business man.

ANNA.

[*Louder.*]

A doctor, I say ! A doctor !

SHOLOM.

[*Aside.*]

My, oh my ! This is enough to make a man crazy ! [*To Hyman and Anna.*] Do you know what? I'll get a business man for you who can cure people, too, or else a doctor who is also a business man. And an end to all this argument. Order some drinks, and let a fellow rinse his throat . . . I'm dry inside from talking with you . . .

> [*Anna rings and cake is served with brandy. Vera enters from the street, her hat still on her head, gloves on her hands, holds a parasol.*]

VERA.

[*To Sholom.*]

Bon jour, monsieur.

SHOLOM.

My name is Sholom, not masee.

VERA.

Ha-ha-ha ! Don't you know ? Bon jour, monsieur, is French for "Good day to you, sir !"

SHOLOM.

A fine time to say "Good day" to anyone, when it's almost night time now . . . Well, good evening to you, Vera. Here's your health, friend Hyman, and yours, Anna ! And here's to Vera's wedding !

VERA.

Ha-ha-ha ! Isn't that droll now ! What are you doing here, anyway, Sholom ? Still harping on matches ? Your trouble is all for nothing. You tire your feet in vain.

SHOLOM.

My feet are my own, and nobody else's.

VERA.
[*Convulsed with laughter*.]

Ha-ha-ha ! Ha-ha-ha !

ANNA.

My daughter, what do you mean by laughing like that ?

HYMAN.

Yes, what do you mean ?

VERA.
[*To her mother*.]

Isn't he the comical looking thing ? Ha-ha-ha ! Where did you find this droll fellow ? What's the matchmaker doing here, I'd like to know !

ANNA.

What's the matchmaker doing ? Making matches, of course ! What do you think ?

VERA.

Matching off whom, I'd like to know ?

HYMAN.

And you ask that ! Whom do you think he's
making a match for, — me ?

ANNA.

They're choosing a husband for you, Vera dear.

VERA.

What do you mean, choosing a husband for me ?
When it comes to choosing a husband, I can speak
for myself ! [*Taking off her gloves.*] What husband
has been proposed, for example ?

ANNA.

A doctor.

HYMAN.

A business man, I say !

ANNA.

[*Loudly.*]

A doctor, and not a business man !

SHOLOM.

[*Nods assent.*]

A doctor, not a business man.

HYMAN.

[*Loudly.*]

A business man, and not a doctor !

SHOLOM.

A business man, and not a doctor.

ANNA.

[*Louder.*]

A doctor !

SHOLOM.

Doctor.

HYMAN.

[*Louder.*]

A business man !

SHOLOM.

[*Exhausted and perplexed.*]

A business man. [*Aside.*] There you go ! The
vaudeville's commencing all over again. [*Aloud.*]
Listen, I've got a plan. ! Let's put it up to the
young lady herself ! [*To Vera.*] Tell us, my good
young lady, which do you prefer, a doctor or a
business man ?

VERA.

You're a boor.

SHOLOM.

A what ?

VERA.

A big boor.

SHOLOM.

I believe you're mistaken, young lady. I'm a matchmaker, not a bear. And what's more, let me tell you I have young men to suit all tastes, and can give you your pick of the best. That's who I am ! I can give you a business-like doctor or a doctor-like business man. The decision is left entirely to you, entirely to you.

VERA.

[*Choking with laughter.*]

Ha-ha-ha ! . . . A business-like doctor or a doctor-like business man ! Ha-ha-ha ! . . .

SHOLOM.

[*Aside.*]

The girl's suspiciously jolly, she is . . . [*Aloud.*] Your health, friend Hyman ! Your health, Mrs. Krendelman ! And Heaven grant us a wedding very soon.

ANNA.

Why don't you say something, my daughter ? Tell your father, — that tyrant, that despot, —

tell him clearly that you'll have a doctor, and not a business man.

SHOLOM.

Yes, a doctor, and not a business man.

HYMAN.

I tell you she'll marry a business man and not a doctor !

SHOLOM.

Yes, a business man, and not a doctor.

ANNA.

[*Loudly.*]

A doctor ! A doctor !

SHOLOM.

Yes, a doctor.

HYMAN.

[*Loudly.*]

A business man, a business man !

SHOLOM.

[*Exhausted.*]

Yes, a business man.

ANNA.

[*Stamping her feet.*]

A doctor ! A doctor ! A doctor !

SHOLOM.

Yes, a doctor ! A doctor ! A doctor ! Here's
your health, friend Hyman, and yours, Mrs.
Krendelman !

VERA.

[Still laughing.]

Ha-ha-ha ! A doctor ! A doctor ! A doctor !

ABRAM.

[From within.]

A doctor ! A doctor !

*[The door leading to the kitchen opens, and
Slottke comes running in, frightened out
of her wits, holding in one hand a duster and
in the other a towel. Immediately behind
her runs Breine the cook, holding a handkerchief and smelling salts.]*

SLOTTKE.

A doctor ? Who wants the doctor ? Which
doctor do you want ? I'll run and get him right
away !

BREINE.

Oh me ! I'm done for ! I've been struck by a
thunderbolt ! What is the matter here ? Has
somebody fainted ? Who's fainted ? Who needs
the doctor ?

[Vera is convulsed with laughter.]

ANNA.

[*Pushing the servants roughly aside.*]
May all the evils of bad dreams descend on your
heads, your hands and your feet ! Out of here, you
good-for-nothings! Out with you, you dunder-
heads, you trash !

[*The servants, in their haste to get out of the
way, stumble into Sholom.*]

SHOLOM.

By Heaven, before these people make up their
minds between yes and no a fellow can suffer a
broken neck . . . A house full of crazy people ! . . .
Upon my faith, what they all need is a doctor . . .
Yes, siree, as much as life itself they need a doctor !
A doctor !

CURTAIN

SHOLOM ASH

SINCE the death of Isaac Leib Perez early in 1915, the mantle of the greatest of Yiddish writers has fallen upon the shoulders of Sholom Ash and with the death of Sholom Aleichem, in May, 1916, Ash became the most popular Jewish author as well.

Ash was born about thirty-five years ago, near Warsaw, the Mecca of Jewish literary men. Thither he went at the age of nineteen, and at twenty-four made for himself a reputation with the first chapters of *"The Town"* and a drama *"Returned."* He has been called the Jewish *de Maupassant* (such characterizations are frequent and natural to a literature that seeks its better standards outside of its own pale) but such a comparison is applied to him only as regards his tales. As a dramatist he has won the lasting friendship of the great producer Max Rheinhardt, who made a success in Berlin, at the *Deutsches Theater*, of a German translation of Ash's *"God of Vengeance."*

Ash is a person of broad and deep culture. He reads some half-dozen languages with ease, is a passionate lover of art, philosophy and nature, and is unceasingly productive in all literary forms. To him, *Hamlet* is the greatest of all plays, and one writer has said that from the ghost scene in this play Ash can trace Maeterlinck and all the mystics.

He has been accused of erotomania, and much of his work would seem to justify the accusation, although wrong inferences are easily drawn. Such a play as *"Jephthah's Daughter,"* with its dramatization of the sex impulse, is despite its monotonous sincerity possessed of a certain elemental power, and is essentially moral. *"The God of Vengeance"* is an impressive, if overdrawn study in the retribution visited upon parents who own a brothel which finally corrupts their own daughter. Ash's drunkards, prostitutes and mysterious women are parts of a whole, not ends in themselves.

He is still a young man, however. It is not at all impossible that his real work has not yet commenced. His latest play is entitled "A String of Pearls," and was suggested by the European War.

Two of Ash's one-act plays are presented in this volume.

"Winter" requires little comment. It is another instance of the self-sacrificing Jewish sister. A comparison of this play with Pinski's *"Forgotten Souls"* helps reveal the difference between Ash and Pinski as dramatists.

The effect of *"The Sinner,"* even upon the

reader who is not intimately acquainted with the superstitions which, in one form or another, are current among the less educated of all races, is that of a blind power. We cannot deny to the writer a certain Greek strength, even if after a first or second reading we are puzzled as to his meaning. It is easy for the religious to interpret the play as being orthodox; the advanced may see in it a certain sympathy for the mysterious woman in black.

Such indecisive symbolism as this dramatic episode reveals is characteristic of Jewish taste both in reading and in the theatre. The Jewish temperament, especially when not yet sophisticated by contact with world-literature, is naturally given to a love of mysticism, symbolism and allegory, as may be expected from its Oriental origin. This temperamental leaning to the mystic and the symbolic is strongly shown not only in the best works in poetry and the tale, but in several ways expresses itself in drama. Many Yiddish plays, to the Western mind, would thus seem to lack climax, whereas the truth is that the Jewish reader or spectator regards the work as a picture, rather than a progress. Indeed, the regular name for the popular Yiddish Broadway melodramas (which have taken over the American recipe, thrills, climaxes and all) is still *Lebensbild*, a picture from life.

To a public that has learned to appreciate Maeterlinck, however, *The Sinner* should present little difficulty. It is useful also to recall, in connection with this play, its author's predilection for *Hamlet*.

WINTER

A Drama in One Act

By SHOLOM ASH

PERSONS

DEBORAH, *a widow*, (60).

ROMA, *her elder daughter*, (32).

ULKA, *the younger daughter*, (20).

MRS. GROSBERG, *a matchmaker, a frequent caller,* (40).

JUDAE, *a poor neighbor*, (40).

SHPRINTZE, *Deborah's cook.*

GOLDBERG, *a young man* [*Behind the scene*].

The action takes place in a small village, situated up North, behind the mountains.
A cloudy winter's day, near noontime.

124

WINTER

SCENE: *Deborah's home. An old house of genteel provincial type. A long, narrow room, occupied by the girls. The furniture is already outworn. It consists of two beds, at the right, covered with white quilts; in front of each bed a mirror, and between, an old, wide wardrobe. At the left, two windows, curtained at the lower halves. Through the top of the windows, in the distance, may be seen a high, snow-bedecked mountain. Between the windows is an old dresser, covered with a crocheted cloth upon which are placed bric-a-brac, porcelain plates, etc. On the wall above is a clock which has stopped. Around about are displayed illustrations which have been clipped from various publications. Glass shelves, here and there, contain the girls' knick-knacks. To the right, a door leading to the parlor. In the background, a door with a white curtain, which leads to an outer room. To the right of this door, a wide blackened stove in front of which is a decrepit sofa. The scene in general impresses one with a sense of Deborah's refinement.*

Roma and Ulka are sitting on the sofa, absorbed in reading.

DEBORAH.

[*An aged woman of earnest aspect. She wears pince-nez and is dressed in a thick,*

*black gown.   Paces up and down the room,
her arms hanging loosely by her side.   She
is engrossed in thought.*]

ROMA.

[*A tall woman, her hair combed well back on
her forehead.   She is wrinkled about the
eyes and mouth.   Wears a black gown and
is wrapped in a heavy shawl.   Her eyes are
glued fast to the book.*]

ULKA.

[*A lively maiden.   She wears a blouse, and
is sitting next to Roma.   From time to
time she looks up from her reading.   For a
long while the three continue as above.*]

JUDAH.

[*An emaciated fellow in a torn coat.   Steals
into the room, trembling with the cold, and
makes for the stove, behind the sofa, where
he warms himself.*]

ULKA.
[*Looks up from the book, surprised.*]
Ah, Judah . . .
[*Turns back to her page.*]

DEBORAH.

[*Turning around, and seeing Judah.*]
Is that you, Judah ? Well, what's the news ? . . .

JUDAH.

[*From behind the stove.*]
News ? What news can there be ? — He who
has anything to eat, eats. He who hasn't, goes
hungry.

DEBORAH.

That's so. [*Resumes her pacing to and fro.*]
Hasn't any business showed up yet ?

JUDAH.

Business ? Who talks business today, when it's
impossible to leave the village or to get into it
from outside !

ULKA.

[*Looking up.*]

Isn't it dreadful !

DEBORAH.

They say that a great sleigh has been sent out,
with a gang of men to clear the road.

JUDAH.

Much they'll be able to do ! The wind, over
night, blew down from the mountains and piled
the snow way up high. Zorach was just telling

us at the synagogue that he wanted to go to town this morning and he was nearly buried in the snow.

ULKA.

Isn't that dreadful !

[*A prolonged silence.*]

SHPRINTZE.

[*At the door.*]

What shall I cook for dinner ?

DEBORAH.

I haven't the slightest notion. [*To Ulka, who is staring about vacantly.*] What shall she cook for dinner ?

ULKA.

What's that to me ?

[*Resumes her reading.*]

DEBORAH.

[*To the cook.*]

Cook anything that you have handy.

SHPRINTZE.

Potatoes ?

DEBORAH.

Let it be potatoes, then. [*To Roma.*] Let's see, I don't think you're very fond of potatoes, are you ?

[*Roma doesn't answer. The cook leaves.
Pause. Deborah walks slowly about the
room, her hands at her side. Roma reads
on.*]

ULKA.
[*She stares about aimlessly, then suddenly
jumps up and looks around.*]
How late is it, I wonder ? [*Nobody makes reply.
She looks at the clock.*] Fine clock you've got here.
It never goes.

[*Enter Mrs. Grosberg. A thin, tall woman.
Wisps of hair show from under her wig,
around which she wears a black ribbon.
Her clothes show signs of once having been
costly, even as her general appearance reveals an air of lost prestige. An artificial
smile plays upon her features.*]

MRS. GROSBERG.
Good morning ! I see the children are hugging
the stove. What else can you do in a little village
like this ? Outside my house, — winter. Inside
my house, winter . . . So I stepped in to see you
for a while, Deborah.

DEBORAH.
[*Seeing Mrs. Grosberg, she stops where she is.
For a moment she looks at her daughters, in
fright. Speaks with assumed cheerfulness.*]

Mrs. Grosberg ! How glad I am to see you ! Tell me, how are you getting along ?

MRS. GROSBERG.

[*Goes near the window.*]

How should I be getting along ? — Bad weather outside.

ROMA.

[*Upon Mrs. Grosberg's entrance she has become more than ever absorbed in the book. Rises nervously, concealing her perturbation beneath a mask of unconcern. Goes to the dresser, fumbles about for something, then goes back to her place, stealing a glance at Ulka as she passes The latter has blushed a deep red. Roma betrays surprise for a second, then continues her reading, mumbling rather loudly, with strong accent. Finally she gets up and without a word rushes out through the rear door, dragging her shawl along. The shawl drops, but she doesn't stop to pick it up. There is a profound silence. Deborah feigns not to notice it. Mrs. Grosberg looks outisde and talks about the weather . . . Ulka reads on, and finally arises and goes out through the door at the right.*]

DEBORAH.

Why are they running away like that, I wonder ?
What makes them run away ?

MRS. GROSBERG.
[*Pulls her by the sleeve.*]
Never mind.   It's all the better.

DEBORAH.
[*Roused.   Looks at her as if to speak, then
changes her mind.*]

MRS. GROSBERG.
[*With assumed cheerfulness.*]
Do you know ? . . . He's coming . . . The young
man is coming to her . . .

DEBORAH.
[*Surprised and frightened.*]
Who ? Whom do you mean ?

MRS. GROSBERG.

He was told very expressly: a young girl, scarcely
eighteen, slender, beautiful . . . Here [*Feels in her
pocket.*] Schwartzberg writes me that the young
man is on the way.   He'll arrive as an agent, representative of the firm Block and Company . . .

DEBORAH.

Good heavens, in weather like this ?

MRS. GROSBERG.

[*Laughing.*]

What is weather like this, when a fellow is coming for a sweetheart ?

DEBORAH.

[*Not quite understanding her.*]

But so quickly ? So quickly ?

MRS. GROSBERG.

[*Comes close to Deborah.*]

Strike your iron while it's hot . . . When it cools off . . . Deborah — [*Looks her straight in the face.*] Are you going to make the same mistake over again? . . . Haven't you learned a lesson from your elder daughter ?

DEBORAH.

But so soon ! . . . Good God in heaven, what will this come to ?

[*Stands in a dilemma.*]

MRS. GROSBERG.

Deborah, don't lose any time . . . Is the parlor in order ? [*To Judah.*] Call in Shprintze, please. [*Judah goes out.*] Deborah, consider what you're doing.

DEBORAH.

But in the name of heaven, what would you have me do ? Take my child and bury her with my own hands ?

SHPRINTZE.

[*At the door*.]

What do you wish, madam ?

MRS GROSBERG.

My dear Shprintze, is the parlor in order ? Go,
please see that it's all swept out nice and clean.
There are guests coming today. You'll get some
tips.

SHPRINTZE.

Yes, fine guests. There won't be any more of
the kind we used to have . . .

MRS GROSBERG.

. . . Yes there will. The old kind of guests are
going to come again . . . And you'll get the kind
of tips you used to get . . . Come, we've got to
see that things are put in order . . . We have
only two hours.

SHPRINTZE.

[*Looks incredulously at Deborah*.]

Shall we get things ready, madam ?

DEBORAH.

I really —

MRS. GROSBERG.

[*To Shprintze*.]

I tell you yes. [*Makes a sign to her*.] Hurry.

[*The cook leaves*.]

DEBORAH.

[*Near the table. Waits for Mrs. Grosberg to speak.*]

MRS. GROSBERG.

Remember what I'm telling you, Deborah. You mustn't let yourself sacrifice one daughter for the sake of the other. Don't forget that Ulka is twenty years old. A young girl, my friend, is like an apple on the tree. It's beautiful and appetizing as long as it's ripe. Once it gets ripe it must ask for someone to come along and eat it, and say grace over it. If it stays there too long, it begins to decay . . . Deborah, strike the iron while it's hot . . . Don't forget that time and tide wait for no man.

DEBORAH.

But what will become of my elder daughter ?

MRS GROSBERG.

Are you going to let her stand in your way ? Don't let that worry you. It's better so.

DEBORAH.

And what am I to do ?

MRS. GROSBERG.

Nothing. Leave everything to me.

[*Goes out. Returns with Ulka.*]

ULKA.

What do you wish, mama dear ?

MRS. GROSBERG.

There's nothing about this to be ashamed of.
There's nothing to hide, either . . . It's an ack-
nowledged misfortune, and nobody's to blame.
Your sister was very particular. This fellow didn't
suit her, that one didn't, until she was left an old
maid. It's a hard matter to find a good match
now. You can't expect to do much with the two
thousand roubles that your father left you . . .
And until, with God's help, Roma will find a
proper match, a second misfortune can befall
this household . . .

ULKA.

[*Blushing.*]

— Yes, yes, but — but what am I to — ?

MRS. GROSBERG.

Nothing at all. Today a young man is coming
to visit you . . .

ULKA.

[*Frightened.*]

Me ? Roma is older than I !

MRS. GROSBERG.

Nobody can help that. That's a misfortune,
as I said . . . And you oughtn't to suffer on that

account . . . That's life — If you expect to wait
until she's married first, then I'm afraid you'll
have to wait a long, long time . . . Today is your
chance. See to it that you take your opportunity
while you may, and not be left in your sister's
plight. Remember, you've only a dowry of two
thousand roubles . . .

ULKA.

I know nothing at all . . . What does mama
say to all this ?

MRS. GROSBERG.

Your mother ? What can she say, poor woman ?
. . . It's enough of a weight on her shoulders,
either way . . . Both Roma and you are her flesh
and blood. She suffers from both sides . . . But
what can she do, after all, if she can help only one,
and not the other ?

ULKA.

I leave everything to mother. I'll do what she
tells me to.

MRS. GROSBERG.

Your mother'll tell you to go and dress up right
away, for it's getting late, and he'll be here in an
hour.

[*Ulka leaves.*]

DEBORAH.

[*Who has been standing during this conversa-
tion with her arms dropped at her sides.
Suddenly exclaims.*]
What shall I do ? What shall I do ?

MRS. GROSBERG.

What to do ? You see that everything is in
first-class order. See that Ulka is all dressed up,
and hide your elder daughter somewhere or other,
lest he should discover — God forbid ! — that there
is an elder daughter in the family . . . That makes
people imagine things . . . It can spoil matters. . .

DEBORAH.

We used always to hide the younger one when
any young man came calling — now we have to
hide the elder. Poor, poor Roma ! That you
should have been born for this !

MRS. GROSBERG.

That's her luck, poor girl ! . . . And she alone
is to blame . . . Well, I must be going. Deborah,
don't lose any time. It's growing late. [*As she
goes out.*] Deborah, remember, it's a matter of
your child's happiness.

[*Leaves. Deborah is left standing in the
middle of the room, in silent doubt.— Several times she approaches the door, is about*

to turn the knob, and then changes her mind.
Walks rapidly away from the door to the
window.   The door opens, and Roma enters,
humming a tune.   Goes to the dresser as if
in search of something.]

ROMA.

[*To herself.*]

She's already gone.

DEBORAH.

[*Turning suddenly from the window.*]

Tell me, my daughter, once for all, what is the
end of all this going to be ?

ROMA.

[*Stopping where she is.*]

How is it that this seems to bother you so much
today ? Has that old thing been in here again to
fill your ears with her talk ? I'll slam the door in
her face next time she comes !

[*She is about to leave the room in a huff.*]

DEBORAH.

[*At her heels, calling.*]

Roma ! Roma ! I want to tell you something.

ROMA.

[*Turns on the threshold.*]

What is it you wish to say ?

[*Awaits her mother's reply anxiously. Finally
she sits down upon the sofa nearby.*]

DEBORAH.

Tell me, what shall I do ? What shall your
unhappy mother do ?

ROMA.

[*Gazes silently upon her mother.*]

What do you want of me ? Am I a burden here ?
Then I'll go out and earn my own living.

DEBORAH.

Woe is me ! You know right well what's the
matter. What's the use of all this talk ? — But
I am your mother, after all. My heart is torn
with pity —

ROMA.

[*With feigned laughter.*]

Pity . . . But I beg you, mother, don't waste
any pity on me . . . [*Pause. Then, with anger.*]
Good God, I don't know . . . [*Stops. Suddenly
continues.*] What right has anyone to pity me ?
. . . Who's asking any one to meddle in my affairs ?
I'm satisfied. I don't care to marry — Then
whose business is it ?

DEBORAH.

I'm your mother. After all is said and done,
I can't look on without my heart breaking.

ROMA.

[*Shouting.*]

But if I don't care, who should bother about it ?

DEBORAH.

But what can I do ? It's breaking my heart,
I tell you. How can I help it, when I see you, a
girl of thirty, sitting around the house and . . .

ROMA.

[*Interrupting.*]

Why should that bother anybody ? Why ? I
simply don't care to marry — it's nobody's business.

DEBORAH.

But remember. [*Comes near to Roma and whispers to her.*] And Ulka ? . . .

ROMA.

[*Aloud.*]

Who's preventing her from getting married ?

DEBORAH.

You, you !

ROMA.

I ! . . Well then, I yield my place to her.
    [*Is lost in thought. Takes up the book nearby
    and glances over its pages.*]

DEBORAH.

[*At her wit's end. Several times she is about to approach Roma, then retreats. Finally she sits down in a corner, and talks to herself.*]

Unhappy mother that I am ! Good God in heaven, what shall I do ? Whither shall I turn ? [*She looks at Roma. Roma, engrossed in her thoughts, makes no response. For a long while not a word is said. Suddenly sounds of activity are heard in the next room. Judah's cheerful voice is giving orders. "Put the oleander near the window" . . . "The curtain is hiding the mirror" . . . Roma looks at her mother, as if for an explanation of the house-cleaning. Deborah looks out of the window, avoiding her daughter's glance. Finally she speaks.*] Terrible weather outside. [*In a tremulous voice.*] I can't understand why we don't get a letter from uncle.

ROMA.

[*Does not reply. After a while she arises, goes over to the dresser, looks for something and tries to hide her emotions by murmuring a tune.*]

"The sun sinks low in the West, in a fiery sky, in a fiery sky . . . "

DEBORAH.

[*Suddenly, in a weary, tearful voice.*]

Daughter, tell me, am I not your mother ? [*Her*

voice is choked with tears.] Or can it be that I don't know . . .

[*She weeps bitterly.*]

ROMA.

Mother, what do you want of me ? . . . Ah ! . . .
[*She leaves the dresser, seizes the book which
has been left on the table, and takes it with
her to her place on the sofa. Affects deep
interest in the book.*]

DEBORAH.

Why are you playing make-believe with me ?
As if I were a total stranger to you . . . Isn't your
trouble my trouble ? . . . Ulka is growing up, fair
of stature People have come to talk matches.
Day after day goes by . . . Time flies . . . She's
getting older; she's twenty already. Why, a girl
is usually a wife at that age. What can I, a poor
widow, do ? God in heaven, what shall I do ?

ROMA.

[*As if reading from the book.*]
They want to marry her off already.

DEBORAH.

And how about yourself ? What will the end be ?

ROMA.

[*With feigned laughter.*]

What shall it be ? I'll live and I'll die.

DEBORAH.

What kind of life do you call that ? Sitting by
the stove day and night, reading books. What
good are the books, anyway ? You're wasting your
life with tales about other people . . . To what
purpose ? To what good ? . . . I spoke to you
about it, I warned you; not only once, nor twice —
"Roma, Roma," I said to you, "don't let your
opportunities go by !" . . . And you would talk
with this fellow, go out walking with that one,
until a wretch came along who made you all kinds
of glowing promises. . .You were as fresh as a rose
then. And they came along to breathe your perfume and leave . . . Then the rose lost its bloom
and its perfume evaporated . . . Every girl has her
season; once it passes, she is lost . . . I warned you,
but you wouldn't listen. What could I, your
unhappy mother, do ?

ROMA.

Then the upshot of all this is that you want me
to get married ? — Very well, then. I'll get married. She's been here already. They're putting
the house in order. There's a prospective bride-
groom coming today. — Very well — I'll not ask

who he is — I'll not even look at him to see whether
I like him or not — I'm satisfied. I'll marry first,
if you wish it.

> [*Secretly glad at the opportunity, having mis-*
> *taken Deborah's intention, and being un-*
> *aware that the young man is coming to visit*
> *not her, but Ulka.*]

DEBORAH.

> [*Frightened.*]

But . . . my daughter ! . . .

ROMA.

Very well, very well, since you desire it . . .
It makes no difference to me whatever . . . I'll
marry right away . . . Once and for all you'll stop
bothering me . . . I'm satisfied. I'll go and dress
up right away . . . Where's my gown ? . . . I'll
be just as meek as you wish, as long as you say so . .
[*Runs into the other room.*] But remember, don't
find any fault with me afterwards.

DEBORAH.

> [*In anxious dilemma.*]

Good heavens, what am I going to do now ?
> [*A short silence. It grows dark. Ulka comes*
> *running in, wearing a new silk blouse, not*
> *yet buttoned.*]

ULKA.

Mamma, please button my blouse.

DEBORAH.

[*Approaches her with great tenderness.*]
Come, my darling. Let me help you dress.
Your bridegroom's coming today. Poor little
fatherless child.

ROMA.

[*From the other room.*]
What kind of dress shall I put on, mother?
My reception gown?

[*Deborah makes no reply. Continues fixing
up Ulka.*]

ULKA.

Mamma, Roma's calling you.

DEBORAH.

That's all right, my darling. Never mind. May
Heaven bring you honor and happiness.

ROMA.

[*From within.*]
Where's Ulka? Let her help me dress. [*Looks
on the stage, but it is quite dark, and she does not
recognize Ulka.*] Who's there?

[*No reply, as if neither Deborah nor Ulka had
noticed her.*]

DEBORAH.

[*Continuing with Ulka.*]

Wait a moment, dear. Your father — may his soul rest in peace — left me a string of pearls to put around your neck when a prospective bride-groom should come, so that you might find favor in his eyes.

ROMA.

[*She has grasped the situation, and sees that the young man is coming for Ulka, not her. For a moment she is overcome. The silk shawl drops from her hand. At first she wishes to steal out of the room unnoticed, but that is impossible. She goes over very quietly to Deborah and Ulka, and speaks in a soft voice.*]

Allow me, mother. I'll dress her for the bride-groom.

[*The mother yields Ulka to Roma, and goes out. Ulka, her head bowed in shame, tries to follow her mother. Roma restrains her.*]

ROMA.

Why should you feel ashamed before me, sister dear ? . . . I know all about it . . . Don't be afraid on my score . . . Don't be ashamed . . . Aren't you my sister ? Isn't your happiness my happiness . . . my — happiness ?

ULKA.

[*Stands confused, undecided.*]

ROMA.

Come, sister, let me comb up your hair. [*Ulka kneels before her, and Roma begins to comb her sister's hair.*] Your hair, sister, is beautiful, silken, and black as the night. . . There is such an air of refinement about you . . . You'll make a stunning bride.
[*Braids Ulka's hair.*]

ULKA.

[*Suddenly jerks herself away from Roma, then falls upon her sister's bosom and weeps bitterly.*]

ROMA.

[*Lifting Ulka's head, and feigning laughter.*]
You dear little fool, you, what are you crying about ? Because you're going to marry ? Just the contrary ! You should be happy !

[*Ulka embraces Roma with greater vehemence and breaks into sobbing, which continues for some time. Roma meanwhile straightens out Ulka's hair. Sleighbells are heard outside. Roma pulls Ulka up and hastily finishes dressing her . . . Footsteps are heard outside.*]

GOLDBERG.

[*Within.*]

I have the honor to present myself — My name is Goldberg. I represent the firm Block and Company.

DEBORAH.

[*Within.*]

Highly honored . . . [*Footsteps are heard, as if people are passing from one room to another. The door at the right opens. A stream of light is cast on the darkened stage. Deborah's head may be seen at the door. Deborah continues.*] Ulka, allow me.

[*Ulka looks at Roma.*]

ROMA.

[*Wipes the tears from Ulka's eyes, and pushes her towards the door.*]

Go . . . Go . . . Go . . .

[*Ulka makes no resistance. Goes in through the door at the right and closes it behind her. The stage is again left in darkness.*]

ULKA.

[*Within.*]

I'm very much pleased to meet you.

[*Someone closes the shutters from the outside . . . The stage becomes darker still . . . Through the interstices of the shutters*

*stream red beams of the setting sun. After
a short while Judah comes in from the rear
door.*]

JUDAH.

[*Sees Roma and is about to step back. Coughs
to attract her attention, then goes behind the
stove to warm up.*]

ROMA.

[*Seeing Judah, she makes believe looking for
something. Then, with a light step, she
goes toward the rear room, affecting only
then to notice Judah.*]

Ah, Judah ! Well, how is it outside ?

JUDAH.
[*Rubbing his hands.*]

It's getting awful cold . . .

CURTAIN

THE SINNER

Drama in One Act

By SHOLOM ASH

PERSONS.

THE TOWN RABBI.

FIRST DAYON, *Synagogue Judge.*

SECOND DAYON.

THE GABBAI OF THE CHEVRA KADISHA, *President of the Burial Society.*

ELDER GRAVEDIGGER.

YOUNGER GRAVEDIGGER.

FIRST, SECOND, THIRD, FOURTH, FIFTH AND SIXTH PERSONS IN THE CROWD.

AN OLD JEW.

THE BEADLE.

A WOMAN IN A BLACK VEIL.

A BEGGAR.

A CROWD OF JEWISH MEN, WOMEN AND YOUNGSTERS.

THE SINNER

SCENE: *A Jewish cemetery in a small town in Russian-Poland. Surrounding the cemetery is a low, dilapidated wooden fence. Here and there stand stunted trees with thick foliage, in whose shadows half tombstones arise from the tall-growing wild grass. In the middle of the graveyard an enclosure, grown over with trees; nearby stands an old Jew, in silent prayer. To the right there is a tumbledown hut with two crude windows that face the burial-ground. Behind the hut a dark gate, in front of which loom two tall, black posts. On the posts are nailed tin plaques, inscribed in Hebrew, with prayers for the dead.*

Before the hut, among the sunken gravestones, graze some goats that are tied to posts which have been driven into the earth. By the door, upon a ramshackle wagon, sits the town beggar, in a ragged cloak that has been thrown over his naked, tanned body. He glares fixedly before him, eyes distended.

On the further side of the fence may be discerned a dark road that winds in and out among the green fields. Far off, in the light of a flaming sunset, appear distinctly the roofs of houses and a high church steeple. Within the fence the diggers are at work upon a new grave, near which lie some boards for the enclosure. To the left, tombstones and trees.

YOUNGER GRAVEDIGGER.
Well, his turn has come at last. He carried his pitcher to the well until —

ELDER GRAVEDIGGER.
We've seen his like before. That fellow who lies over there by the fence, next to the chap that hanged himself, was even worse.

YOUNGER GRAVEDIGGER.
— This one would sit in the cafe on the Day of Atonement, eating roast chicken and butter. *

ELDER GRAVEDIGGER.
With which to feed the worms in his grave.

YOUNGER GRAVEDIGGER.
They didn't find even a praying-shawl in his home for the burial service.

ELDER GRAVEDIGGER.
He was a bachelor, wasn't he ?

YOUNGER GRAVEDIGGER.
Oh, he lived with some woman or other. Gentile, or Jewess. Devil knows whether she was his wife or his mistress.

*A double sin, since fasting is enjoined for atonement day, and the eating of milk-products with meat is against Mosaic Law.

ELDER GRAVEDIGGER.
I shouldn't want to reap the reward of his merits.

YOUNGER GRAVEDIGGER.
And she gave them perfumed soap to wash the corpse with. Perfumed soap !

ELDER GRAVEDIGGER.
Much good his perfumed body will do him, with a soul so unclean !

YOUNGER GRAVEDIGGER.
The burial society refused to carry out his body. She had to hire four pall-bearers. [*He throws up a shovelful of earth, and bones fall out.*]

ELDER GRAVEDIGGER.
Look ! These are bones.
[*Stops digging. Looks closely at the bones.*]

YOUNGER GRAVEDIGGER.
Right you are. Bones.
[*Stops digging and looks at the old man.*]

ELDER GRAVEDIGGER.
Bones. We must put them back. [*They replace the bones, covering them again with earth.*] The grave-yard is moving. This must once upon a time have

been the best location, and now it's near the fence. *
Here we now bury hanged men and thieves. The
place is forgotten, and the fence is built right over
it. The tombstones sink and there isn't a trace of
a grave left.

> [*Darkness comes on, and a cold wind blows
> through the trees. Upon the dark road on
> the further side of the fence approaches the
> burial cortege. The corpse is carried by
> four pall-bearers; behind walks a woman in
> mourning, her face concealed in a black
> veil. Somewhat further behind her follow
> a few inquisitive youngsters. Among these
> is the Gabbai of the Chevra Kadisha, a
> middle-aged person with swarthy face and
> black, thick eyebrows. The people go in
> groups, conversing quietly.*]

YOUNGER GRAVEDIGGER.
They're coming with the corpse.

ELDER GRAVEDIGGER.
We've got to wait for the Gabbai.

> [*The diggers stand up in the grave so as to look
> through the fence, and they beckon to the
> Gabbai.*]

GABBAI.
> [*Sticking his head through the fence.*]

What ? The grave's not ready yet ?

* *i.e.,* The worst location, reserved for suicides, renegades, etc.

ELDER GRAVEDIGGER.

We found human bones as we dug. . . So we filled the grave in again.

GABBAI.

Bones! . . . [*Leaving the fence.*] How do bones come here ?

> [*The black gate opens noisily. The corpse is carried in on the shoulders of the pall-bearers, and placed near the posts. The upper board is removed. The body may be seen behind the black shroud, whence protrude two feet and a head. The woman in black stands near the head, face buried in her hands. She is silent . . . The bearers are about to take up the corpse again, when the voice of the Gabbai is heard.*]

GABBAI

Halt ! Halt !

> [*The crowd, in small groups, stands aloof, now looking at the corpse, now at the woman. There is a subdued whispering. A short silence.*]

FIRST PERSON.

> [*Sarcastically.*]

The corpse waits for its grave. A good omen !

SECOND PERSON.

Hell itself is in no hurry to welcome him.

[*More whispering among the groups. The
woman in black approaches, and is about to
raise the black coverlet from the head of the
corpse.*]

GABBAI.

Don't let her do that ! She mustn't !

THE WOMAN.

[*In Polish.*]

Let me see him only once more.

GABBAI.

[*From within.*]

It is forbidden.

[*The woman goes back to her position at the
head of the corpse. She is silent.*]

FIRST PERSON.

Who is she?

SECOND PERSON.

She came with him from over the border. Nobody can say whether she was his wife or his
mistress, or whether she is Jewish or Gentile. She's
never been seen in a synagogue, or in a church, for
that matter.

THIRD PERSON.

She's the only one left to pray for his soul.

GABBAI.

[*To the gravediggers, indicating a place near the fence.*]

See if you can dig here.

ELDER GRAVEDIGGER.

Near the fellow who hanged himself ?

YOUNGER GRAVEDIGGER.

They'll make a good pair of chums.

[*The diggers commence to dig.*]

FIRST PERSON.

[*Sarcastically.*]

A worthy grave, indeed !

SECOND PERSON.

No worse than he deserved.

THIRD PERSON.

Let him be sure that he remembers his own name when the angel Domai asks it.*

FOURTH PERSON.

He'll talk Polish with the angel.

* The angel's request must be answered with a passage from the Psalms, which sinners cannot remember.

FIFTH PERSON.
He'll offer him a Sabbath-cigarette.*

SIXTH PERSON.
With roast chicken and butter.

THE OLD JEW.
Be merciful.   He's dead now.

A GROUP IN THE CROWD.
It's a shame ! To mock the dead !

[*Silence.*]

YOUNGER GRAVEDIGGER.
My spade slides into the earth altogether too
easily, as if there weren't any earth there at all.

ELDER GRAVEDIGGER.
I'm afraid that —

YOUNGER GRAVEDIGGER.
[*Stops digging.*]
I quit digging right now.

ELDER GRAVEDIGGER.
Me too.

GABBAI
[*From the distance.*]
What's the trouble ?

* Orthodox Jews do not smoke on the Sabbath.

YOUNGER GRAVEDIGGER.

It seems to me that my spade touched a human body.

[*The crowd stirs, and surrounds the grave.*]

GABBAI.

[*Pulling on a pair of brass spectacles, which he takes from a rear-pocket.*]

What can this signify ?

[*The crowd is silent; people look at each other in fright, as if anticipating something. Suddenly a stream of water gushes out of the grave. General commotion. An impressive silence.*]

FIRST PERSON.

[*In terror.*]

The earth refuses to receive him !

SECOND PERSON.

Even Hell has closed its doors to him !

THIRD PERSON.

Good God in Heaven, how awful his sins must be !

[*The crowd shuns the dead man, leaving him alone with the woman in black. She kneels down before the corpse, hiding her face in the black coverlet. The people withdraw.*]

No one interferes with her. There is a
long silence; night comes on. Here and
there, from the crowd come stray sentences:
"What will come of this? What now?

GABBAI.

Send for the Rabbi.

THE GRAVEDIGGERS.

It's getting dark. Have lanterns brought from
the town.

[*Retreating footsteps are heard.*]

FIRST PERSON.

What's to be done?

GABBAI.

My advice is to dig a grave for the dead man
near that of Reb Jehuda.

ELDER GRAVEDIGGER.

What ! Near the grave of Reb Jehuda, — one
of the chosen Thirty-six !*

GABBAI.

The merits of Reb Jehuda will procure for the
corpse its reception into the earth. Near his

* Jewish tradition has it that the world is supported by the
piety of thirty-six saints, who carefully conceal their
sanctity under the guise of some humble occupation.

grave no water will gush forth. The sinner can
escape from hell only with a saint's aid. The
sinner holds tightly to the saint, and through the
saint's good deeds is saved from Gehenna.

PERSONS IN THE CROWD.
And what about Reb Jehuda's honor ?

GABBAI.
Reb Jehuda cared little enough about honor
while alive, and it's of even less moment after
death.

ELDER GRAVEDIGGER.
I don't care to dig his grave near Reb Jehuda's.
[*Flings down his spade.*]

YOUNGER GRAVEDIGGER.
Count me out of it, too.

GABBAI.
[*Tightens his girdle. Goes over to a low stone
which is hidden behind a tree, begins to
sway back and forth as he speaks with
religious fervor.*]
To Him who created the world in six days it is
known that not to offend the honor of Reb Jehuda
do we desire to bury this corpse near him. We
are in doubt and we know not what to do. We

wish to have the sinner acquire merit from lying near the saint.

> [*He takes a spade and commences to dig a grave. Silence.*]

FIRST PERSON.

There is Reb Jehuda's stone, on which for forty years he lay, a hermit, and studied the Torah.

SECOND PERSON.

The stone was worn out in the middle, from the neck of him who lay upon it for forty years.

THIRD PERSON.

When he died they put this stone over his grave as a monument.

FIRST PERSON.

How did this corpse ever earn the honor of resting by the side of Reb Jehuda?

SECOND PERSON.

> [*Sarcastically.*]

He must have performed one good deed in his whole life, and this is his righteous reward!

> [*On the road afar may be seen lights from lanterns. Gradually there may be distinguished men in dark coats, women in shawls, young men carrying lanterns. They enter*

the graveyard, and question one another in subdued voices. "What's the matter?" ... "What's the trouble?" ... Seeing the corpse and the woman in the black veil they are overcome with fright and withdraw to the groups that encircle the grave. Silent suspense.]

GABBAI.

[*Suddenly stops digging.*]

Heavens! I feel that my spade has struck something hard. It can't dig down any further.

PERSONS IN THE CROWD.

[*Greatly excited.*]

Good God in Heaven!

OTHERS IN THE CROWD.

What's going to be done with the corpse?

VOICE.

Better wait till the Rabbi arrives.

SECOND PERSON.

Let the Dayons be sent for!

THIRD PERSON.

A terrible misfortune has been visited upon us all, Father in Heaven!

GABBAI.

Some light over here ! Let's see what's in the grave.

ELDER GRAVEDIGGER.

I advise you not to look.

GABBAI.

[*Clambers up out of the grave, takes a lantern and returns to the grave. With an outcry.*]

There's a stone here !

PERSONS IN THE CROWD.

A stone !

FIRST PERSON.

Reb Jehuda's stone lies flat across the grave and will not permit the corpse to be buried near Reb Jehuda.

SECOND PERSON.

The earth refuses to receive him.

PERSONS IN THE CROWD.

What's to be done with the body ?

FIRST PERSON.

Silence ! The Rabbi is coming !

[*On the road may be seen the lights of large lanterns, which shine upon three old men*

*with white beards and tall fur caps. The
one in the middle, who is the oldest of the
three leans with one hand upon a staff, with
the other upon the Beadle. The latter is
carrying a large lantern. The gate opens;
the three men enter, pass by the corpse, look
in astonishment and fright at the woman,
who is kneeling, then immediately retreat.
They approach the half-dug grave and stand
there reluctantly, as if in a dilemma. Subdued whispering in the crowd, which surrounds the men. Silence.]*

RABBI.

*[After consulting with the Dayons, turns to the
crowd.]*

Friends, we have come to the decision that in
order that this corpse may be placed in a Jewish
grave each one of us must surrender to the dead
man one of our good deeds forever. For my part,
I give him twenty pages' reading of the Commen-
tary Beirochos, from the Talmud.

FIRST DAYON.

I offer him the observance of one Sabbath.

SECOND DAYON.

I present the fasting of one Day of Atonement.

FIRST PERSON.
And I, a chapter of the Biblical Commentaries.

SECOND PERSON.
And I, a week-day morning paper.

THIRD PERSON.
And you can have, from me, a day's reading of the Psalms.

RABBI.
Enough ! [*To the diggers.*] You may resume digging.

> [*The diggers resume digging, and their spades are heard striking against a stone.*]

ELDER GRAVEDIGGER.
The stone simply won't budge.

> [*Silence again overpowers the crowd; the Rabbi and the Dayons consult once more. An atmosphere of terror pervades the place. A quiet sobbing comes from the woman in black.*]

FIRST DAYON.
Can it be that the corpse has desecrated the honor of the saints who dwell in the glory of God's splendor ?

[*Silence.*]

RABBI.

[*Turning to the Dayons, with a hoarse, stacatto voice.*]

Ye who dwell in the glory of God's splendor, perhaps this corpse, during its life, has desecrated your honor. In its name, and in the name of all Israel, I beg forgiveness. Take him with ye. And thou, Reb Jehuda, who wert humble in thy great renown during life, surely wilt thou not be proud in death. Let the good entreat for the evil, and suffer this corpse to repose near thee.

[*Impressive silence. Restrained sobbing is heard from the woman in black.*]

GABBAI.

[*To the diggers.*]

Go down and see if you can dig now.

[*The gravediggers take a lantern into the grave and start digging once more. There is heard the ring of iron against stone.*]

ELDER GRAVEDIGGER.

The stone refuses to budge. Wherever the spade goes it strikes the stone.

[*The Rabbi and the Dayons hold another consultation, in subdued tones. There is a murmuring in the crowd, then a silent expectancy.*]

RABBI.
> [*Turning to the earth.*]

Earth, mother of all, out of whom cometh all
and to whom all returneth — if this corpse, while
living, sinned against thee, I ask thee forgiveness
in his name and in the name of all Israel.   For out
of dust cometh man, and to dust returneth.

> [*Deep silence.   The diggers resume their work,
> and soon the ring of the iron spades upon the
> stone is heard again.*]

ELDER GRAVEDIGGER.
The stone doesn't budge.

> [*Silent horror grips the crowd.   The suppressed
> sobbing of the woman in black continues.*]

FIRST DAYON.
> [*After a long pause.*]

Can it be that the corpse was guilty of blas-
phemy ?

SECOND DAYON.
Maybe it doesn't belong to this cemetery ?

RABBI.
> [*After a short deliberation.*]

Where is the caretaker of the grounds ?

ELDER GRAVEDIGGER.
What do you wish ?

RABBI.

Have some wood brought; build a fire in the graveyard. Place in the fire seven bricks. [*To the crowd.*] If the bricks crack, that will signify that his Judaism has cracked likewise . . . in that case his corpse does not belong to this graveyard, and the earth will not take him in.

> [*Wood is brought, and a fire is made, near the dead body. Seven bricks are placed in the fire, which flames up and illumines the surrounding crowd. Another flash reveals the corpse and the woman in black kneeling beside it. A long pause of suspense. Suddenly the crack of a splitting brick is heard.*]

PERSONS IN THE CROWD.

A brick has cracked !

RABBI.

Only one.

> [*Another crack is heard.*]

PERSONS IN THE CROWD.

Another !

RABBI.

That makes only two.

> [*The remaining bricks, with the exception of one, crack in turn, and fall out of the flames.*

*Out of the awed silence of the crowd now and
then breaks forth from a frightened onlooker:
"God in Heaven!" . . . "Almighty Father."*

PERSONS IN THE CROWD.

Good God above ! What can the corpse have
been guilty of ?

RABBI.

One brick still remains whole.

PERSONS IN THE CROWD.

And that one's cracking now !

[*Pause.*]

SECOND PERSON.

It's cracking in every direction. It'll split in
a moment.

PERSONS IN THE CROWD.

[*Terror-stricken.*]

This very second ! Now ! Now !

RABBI.

It hasn't split yet.

[*Silence.*]

FIRST PERSON.

The pieces of the brick hold together as if the
fire fused them.

FIRST DAYON.
It is not so easy for a Jewish soul to depart from the path of Judaism.

SECOND DAYON.
He surely must have endured much sorrow before he came to that point.

RABBI.
Even as the brick in the flames, so did his soul burn in the flames of life. [*The fire dies out gradually; only embers remain. The brick remains whole. The crowd gathers about, in awed silence. The Rabbi and the Dayons approach the fire and examine the stone. The Rabbi then turns to the open grave and speaks in quiet, solemn voice.*] Earth, you must receive him. For he has, in spite of everything, remained a Jew, and belongs in this cemetery. And ye other graves, whether ye so will it or not, must grant him a place among ye.

GABBAI.
[*To the diggers.*]
Dig.
[*The diggers commence digging again.*]

ELDER GRAVEDIGGER.
The stone crumbles at the touch of my spade.

RABBI.

[*To the Beadle.*]

Go over to the corpse and say to it: You are not
this woman's husband and she is not your wife.

THE BEADLE.

[*Tightens his girdle, approaches the corpse
and says:*]

You are not this woman's husband.   She is not
your wife.

[*The Gabbai and a man from the crowd remove
the corpse from the woman, who remains
kneeling at the spot.   The body is taken from
its litter and it is lowered, with its black
shroud, into the grave.   The Gabbai breaks
an earthen pot, placing the shards upon the
eyes and the mouth of the corpse.*]

GABBAI.

[*To the corpse.*]

I seal the eyes which have gazed upon evil, and
the mouth which has uttered it.

[*The grave is filled in.   One by one the crowd
leaves, some taking lanterns along.   Only
the elder gravedigger and the woman in
black remain.   The former, by the light of
his lantern and the glow of the fire's dying
embers, nails a board above the newly made
grave.   Beyond the fence, on the dark road,*]

may be seen the figures of the retreating
crowd, and the lantern lights which gradually
grow dimmer.

ELDER GRAVEDIGGER.
[*Having fulfilled his duty, stands for a moment*
over the grave, addressing it.]
May thy sinful soul rest in peace
[*Takes his lantern and leaves. The scene is*
left in darkness, save for the dying embers
of the fire. By their pale light the woman
in black may be seen approaching the grave
as if treading upon hallowed ground. She
throws her black veil upon the grave. From
afar are discerned the last glimmerings of
the lanterns.]

SLOW CURTAIN

PEREZ HIRSCHBEIN

Perez Hirschbein is a young man of some
thirty-five years. Born the son of a poor miller
in a small Russian town he became known at
twenty-five as a writer of drama in Hebrew, later
in Yiddish.

He has been much influenced by the French
symbolists and mystics, as is attested by the
dialogue of his plays and the beauty of his prose-
poems. In fact, some of his one-act plays incline
so strongly to the mystic that the very element
which adds to them perhaps, as poetry, injures
them as actable drama. In these plays Hirschbein
is first of all the prose-poet, and dramatist in a
secondary sense only.

In such a drama as *"Einsame Welten"* [Solitary
Worlds] during the short course of the play there is
little, if any, dialogue. The characters speak to
us by speaking only to themselves. One curses
his fate in a withering invective that pales into
mere scolding when translated; another has gone
mad over Talmudical disputation, and repeats
his fixed idea with a mechanical simplicity that
overwhelms; a young child draws designs upon the
floor and talks about the music upstairs as if it

were (as indeed it is) in another world, and so on. Here is a cellar full of people, yet each is a world unto himself. Or again, examine the beautiful piece which the author, perhaps feeling its essentially non-dramatic qualities, has entitled an idyll, *"Bebele."* The story of the play is touching: the superstitious penance which a mother takes upon herself for her daughter's welfare. Yet its dramatic vision, so to speak, is too weak to endure the glare of the footlights. So, too, the charming playlet called *"The Storm,"* with its illustrative sub-title: Once Upon A Time the Jews Reveled.

In such a play, however, as *"In Der Finster"* [In The Dark], by which Hirschbein is represented in this volume, the author succeeds admirably in fusing plot, poetry and symbolism into a dramatic unity where the tragedy of poverty and shattered illusions is depicted with a poignancy and power that entitle this one-act play to a place among the best of its genre in any tongue.

IN THE DARK

A Dramatic Study in One Act

By PEREZ HIRSCHBEIN

PERSONS.

FAIVE, *a man who performs odd jobs on the street.*

PESHKE, *his daughter.*

FAYGE, *blind mother of Faive.*

BAYNISH, *an old porter.*

ABRAM, *a young chimney-sweep.*

IN THE DARK

SCENE: *A winter evening. Faive's home. Two long and narrow rooms in a deep cellar. As the stage grows gradually lighter there may be seen, in the room of the foreground at the right, an oven. On the floor, black pots and similar utensils. To the left, windows placed deep in the walls. Broken-down furnishings. In the background, the other room. Black pipes lead from a small iron stove to the chimney in the room of the foreground.*

The stage is dark. For a while it remains empty. From the rear room are heard Fayge's footsteps, accompanied by groans and sighs.

FAYGE.

[*Gropes around.*]

She's out, it seems. I just dozed off a bit, and out she skipped . . . The oven's cold. The fire died out before it had a chance to warm up . . . And here it is freezing again . . . Hu, hu . . . Dark . . . Doesn't seem to be anything burning. [*Feels her way about.*] Peshke ! Eh ? . . . She's out. Could she have left the door open ? It's cold . . . No, the door's closed. What a life ! What a life ! Hu, hu . . . Well, there's some of me left yet, at least. [*The door opens, and someone enters.*] Who is that? Eh? Who is it? . . . Baynish?

BAYNISH.

Good evening. It's I.

FAYGE.

Baynish?

BAYNISH.

Yes, Baynish . . . Why is it dark here?

FAYGE.

What do I need light for? I'm looking for Peshke. She was here just a moment ago. I dozed off . . . Is it very dark here?

BAYNISH.

Very. It's cold in your house. I thought I could warm up here a little.

FAYGE.

It's terrible cold. What do you say?

BAYNISH.

Something awful. Simply unbearable.

FAYGE.

Did you earn anything?

BAYNISH.

I didn't even untie my rope ... It's cold.
Didn't you make any fire today ?

FAYGE.

Certainly.   What a question !

BAYNISH.

With sticks, eh ?

FAYGE.

With big logs.   And I sawed them with my own
hands.

BAYNISH.

It's awful cold.

FAYGE.

Isn't it too dark for you ?

BAYNISH.

Can't see a thing.

FAYGE.

There ought to be a little lamp on the table over
there.

[*Both go into the back room.*]

BAYNISH.

Here it is.   Now we need some matches.

FAYGE.

Look on the mantel.

BAYNISH.

By the chimney?

FAYGE.

Sometimes they're there . . . She simply can't
stay in the house. Maybe she's sleeping somewhere in here. Look around, please, and see if
you can spy her.

BAYNISH.

Who?

FAYGE.

Peshke. She stays home. Walks around barefoot.

BAYNISH.

Can't see anyone. It's dark . . . Like a dungeon.

FAYGE.

Then I must have slept for a long time. It's a
habit with me these days. My eyelids just drop
at times. When I could see, the least bit of noise
would wake me right away . . . And now, God be
praised, blindness on top of my other cares. You
didn't find her?

BAYNISH.

I don't know where to look . . . What a terrible cold day it's been. When you don't earn a cent it's bitter indeed.

FAYGE.

She's out, all right. Simply can't stay inside. Somebody was here during the day. They whispered into each other's ears. Could it have been Abram ? She wouldn't tell me.

BAYNISH.

I'd make her tell me, all right ! What's Faive doing about it ? And the rope ? Why do you spare the rope ?

FAYGE.

It's painful to twist a rope into young skin. Her body's too delicate for the rope. She won't do anything. She doesn't want to put the yoke around her neck. Am I to hang it on her ? I can't see what's going on in the world. It's soon thirty years. The street must look altogether different now . . .

BAYNISH.

But how can a girl leave her grandmother in the dark ? Faive must know of this. I'll lend him my rope.

FAYGE.

He has his own rope . . . Hu, hu . . . And I live
on thus in the dark. Blind, yet hankering for
warmth. Hu, hu . . . To beat grown-up children
is the same as beating yourself . . . I knew a mother
who began beating her children even before their
birth . . . She would strike herself with her fists
in the stomach. Couldn't stand the bitter life
within her . . . Her husband nagged her, and she
didn't know upon whom to vent her wrath. She
was beside herself with rage . . . What is the child
to blame ? Peshke is a mere girl. She wants to
have a good time.

BAYNISH.

And for that, maybe I wouldn't give it to her
with the rope !

FAYGE.

And who ever whipped Faive ? Such a mischief, too, — a born mischief ! I had a hard time
bearing him. He wanted to spring out of my
bowels before the time. Stood on his head and
kicked at my heart with his feet . . . Very hard
time bearing him ! He was born — and his yoke
came with him. The yoke, too, I bore within me.

[*The other room becomes light, of a sudden.*]

PESHKE.

[*Enters, with a burning match in her hand.*]

BAYNISH.

Ah ! Here she is ! I didn't know it.

PESHKE.

Show me that rope of yours, Baynish. Into how many knots is it twisted ? [*The match goes out*.] So you'd lend your rope to papa, would you ? Why, you can't even untie it from your neck !

FAYGE.

I thought you were out, somewhere. Light up, my child.

PESHKE.

Where could I go, barefoot, in a cold spell like this ?

BAYNISH.

She must have hid under the table . . . I searched everywhere. Ha, ha ! She heard every word we said. Well, what she heard was all true. Her father is too easy with her.

PESHKE.

Yes, too easy. Too easy.

BAYNISH.

Then he's a fool. Children must be whipped. You've got to give it to them on their bare body !

PESHKE.

You're in a jolly mood, Baynish, — in a jolly mood.

BAYNISH.

There, there. I was fooling. Really, I was only joking.

FAYGE.

You weren't joking at all, Baynish. Sometimes we say things and then we ourselves feel that they're foolish.

BAYNISH.

A child shouldn't be a mill-stone around her father's neck. And if she is, the father ought to beat her.

PESHKE.

Do you think I don't know that you spoke with my father? Baynish imagines that with his ropes he'll help my father bind me.

FAYGE.

Better light a candle.

PESHKE.

I'd just as soon sit in the dark. [*Lights a match.*] If you had children, you'd talk differently. Here he is talking about bringing up children, and he doesn't know what a child is !

BAYNISH.

I'd be merciless. For lighting matches without need I'd break off their fingers for them . . . I'm joking, little fool.

PESHKE.

It's all the same to me whether you're joking or not. My clothes on the wall have rotted from the mould. How much longer will I have to be here ? Till my sides commence to rot ? I don't want to rot alive — what's more, I won't !

[*Lights another match.*]

FAYGE.

Don't waste the matches. Don't. Young folks have no sense. You need wisdom. Foolish child. To be born is to be lost . . . Didn't your mother give birth to you in a cellar ? Much damper than this place . . . The walls were all mouldy, and near the bed they were hung over with sacks. The sacks got rotten. And you laughed, — kicked out your feet and laughed. Some children begin to laugh very early, in the second week, before the mother is out of bed. But once they begin to talk, they laugh no more. They cry.

PESHKE.

I'm not going to cry anymore, now.   No more.

BAYNISH.

Oh, you'll cry yet. You'll bury your head in
your pillow and cry . . . It's warmer over at my
house. Good night. [*Goes out. Silence.*]

PESHKE.

He doesn't even know how to crack a joke.
He talks to papa against me.

FAYGE.

Faive isn't so bad these days. Troubles, my
child, make people unkind. You get angry at
yourself, and curse yourself. Isn't a child part
of a parent's own flesh ?

PESHKE.

But pa can't even stand to see me raise my head.

FAYGE.

His own head, child, is buried ten feet under-
ground. If he ever laughs, I haven't heard it.
Never. Troubles gnaw at him. It's a grave we
live in. I may not see; darkness is everywhere
around me. What difference does it make where
I am ? Above, or below ? No difference, it seems.
Not so. With my blind eyes I can see that I'm

lying in a tomb. If I can't get up, what of it?
Hu, hu . . . You're right, my child, you're right . . .
[*Her voice falters.*] Come to me, my child. With
my blind eyes I see that you are right. My hands
shall give you protection. Your father won't
touch you. I won't let him hit you. I'll tell him.

PESHKE.

What can you have to tell him? I don't know
whether he beats me from love or suffering.

FAYGE.

I'll tell him, my child, that a grown-up girl, —
a grown-up girl should be spared. That she should
be respected. He can't bear to see you go around
idle, my darling. When a man's drowning, even
a straw is too heavy for him to support . . . Where
are you, my child?

PESHKE.

Here I am.

[*She lights a match.*]

FAYGE.

When you strike a light I seem to see the whole
cellar.

PESHKE.

No, you don't see it, grandma, you don't.
Neither of us does.

[*It becomes again dark.*]

FAYGE.

But you see that I notice it's become dark again.

PESHKE.

I'll make it light again for you.

[*Strikes another match.*]

FAYGE.

Too bad. A pity to use up the matches. Certainly I see. I see everything. I see even you. [*After a pause.*] The place is empty. There ought to be some warm water, at least. He'll be frozen when he comes in from the street.

PESHKE.

Warm water ! Warm water ! What will be the good of it ? Come what may. I couldn't stand it, granny, I couldn't stand it any longer. Rather die of hunger than to rot alive. Oh, granny, granny !

[*Throws herself upon Fayge's neck.*]

FAYGE.

It's so long since you worked in the factory, yet you still smell tobacco.

PESHKE.

The odor will stick to me as long as I live. [*Silence. Then, suddenly, in a louder voice, roused.*]

Tell me, grandma, why should a young girl like me be so sad ? I'm lonesome, I feel oppressed ! Shall I have to die of lonesomeness ? If pa should come home and beat me black and blue with his rope, perhaps I'd feel better.

FAYGE.

My child, you're seventeen years old, and I'm seventy. It's hard to close one's eyes for good . . . But once they're closed, it's as if a stone drops from the heart. You suffer in loneliness, and I grope about in the dark.

PESHKE.

Do you think, grandma, that I'm too lazy to work ? No, granny, I'm not ! I'd do anything in the world to make things easier.

[*Silence.*]

FAYGE.

Find some way, my child, to get away from here . . . I made a mistake before. It seemed to me secret conversation, whispering was going on . . . Maybe it was Abram . . . Perhaps he'll take you out of here . . . I talked it over with Baynish. I shouldn't have done so . . .

PESHKE.

Ah, grandma, if you but knew how my heart aches. As if iron teeth gnawed at it. My whole

body grows hot and cold by turns ... And at
times, it's even darker in my eyes than in yours.
Mamma used to tear out my hair. I was small
then and I didn't understand. I just cried, and
couldn't understand. And she would tear out my
hair. Tell me, did it make her feel better to give
me pain ?

FAYGE.

She tore out her own heart. I know, my darling,
how much she loved you. But it was her troubles.
Your mamma died from hunger. She would feed
you with potatoes, and herself would swallow
saliva ... Would swallow her tears ... [*Silence.*]
Your pa will soon come home. He'll be hungry,
and you've prepared no food for him. That'll
make him angry ... A mother can bear everything, a father — nothing. A mother can sacrifice herself before her time, — can bury herself
alive for her child. When you had the pox and
the measles, and your throat became affected, —
Heaven keep us from evil — you didn't hear your
mother weeping over you. But I, my child,
heard her ... With my blind eyes I heard her,
and a fire consumed me. My tears burned, for a
blind person can't weep. Impossible. Wasn't
your mother my daughter-in-law ? ... She was
like a dying candle, and with my blind eyes I saw
how she flickered ... Hu, it's cold ... You say

you're lonely ? Why shouldn't you be ? I can't
see . . . I'm blind. If my eyes were to open, I'd
sob like a child. I'd look at your father and
wouldn't know him. His face must have changed.
When a man beats his grown-up child, his face
must be black with suffering . . . When a man pulls
his only child by the hair . . . my darling, it's
suffering that makes him do it.

[*Silence.*]

PESHKE.

I worked in the factory and just rotted away in
the foul atmosphere. And all around me sat
yellow and green faces. Not a word did they say
. . . Just silence and decay . . . And I, too, kept
silent. But in my heart something tugged, something was breaking. Terror came over me . . .
Granny ! Loneliness overpowered me. It became
awful ! When a candle dies out and melts away . . .
And when human beings melt away and die out,
bend and collapse — it's frightful . . . Tell me,
grandma, am I wrong if I run from fire lest I should
melt away like a candle ? . . . When I see a face
turning yellow like a leaf in autumn, I'm afraid . . .
I feel that I could die . . . It seems that of a sudden
my face has become all wrinkled . . . And my eyes
. . . Oh, granny, I'm afraid to say all that I think
. . . And here at home it's even worse . . . Tell me,
grandma. As you sit here in the cellar, don't you

sometimes feel that the walls are weighing down upon your head, — weighing down and crushing your very bone and marrow together ?

FAYGE.

[*Kisses Peshke.*]

Youth ! Youth ! How sensitive it is to pain ! When I was young, my darling, about your age, and could still see, everything affected me. It hurt. Merciless agony . . . They broke my limbs, while I bit my lips till the blood came — bit them from suffering and didn't utter a sound. I had more strength in those days, more power to suffer in silence . . . Children of today haven't the strength to do that . . . Hu, hu. It's so cold ! . . . Suffering, — nothing but suffering. And no strength to bear it . . .

[*Silence.*]

ABRAM.

[*Enters.*]

Pitch dark in here. Anybody 'round ?

PESHKE.

Come here, Abie !

FAYGE.

We got a-talking, and forgot all about the fire.

ABRAM.

You can't see how sooty my face is in the dark.

PESHKE.

Is it very cold outside ?

ABRAM.

Terrible. Working way up around the chimneys it's still colder. The wind blows from every direction.

PESHKE.

Sometimes you can fall down from up there, too. A sudden gust of wind could push you over.

FAYGE.

People meet their death more often in the streets.

ABRAM.

If feels great to balance yourself on the top of a roof and look down into the street, and see the people bustling. They squirm about here and there and run just as if someone were driving them with a long whip.

PESHKE.

Here, light the lamp. It's there on the table. My feet are cold. I'm barefoot.

[*Abram lights a small lamp on the table. The cellar is peopled with shadows.*]

FAYGE.

Is it light already ?

ABRAM.

Why are you both cuddled up so close together ?

PESHKE.

[*Releases herself from Fayge. Her face is pale, without a trace of gladness.*]

We were keeping each other warm . . . How black you are ! . . . Wash your face . . .

[*She clasps his hand.*]

ABRAM.

[*Looks into her eyes for a long while.*]

I'll wash up . . .

[*Washes himself.*]

FAYGE.

Better make the fire, Peshke. He may bring something from the street that will need cooking.

ABRAM.

There ! Is my face clean now ?

PESHKE.

You're still covered with soot.

[*She hugs his neck.   Pause.*]

FAYGE.

Are you starting the fire?

PESHKE.

[*First whispers something into Abram's ear,
then, looking at her grandmother, says aloud.*]
You say it's very cold outside?

ABRAM.

Very cold and windy.

FAYGE.

Warm up something to eat. Your father'll soon
be here. Don't give him any cause for anger.

PESHKE.

[*Whispers to Abram. He trembles. She releases herself and stands distraught.*]
An empty house. An empty house . . .

ABRAM.

[*Goes over to Peshke and takes her hand.*]

FAYGE.

Has Abram left already?

ABRAM.

No, I'm here yet.

[*Whispers to Peshke.*]

PESHKE.

*[Shakes "no" with her head.   Then aloud to
Fayge.]*

They melted away just like candles in front of
a flame, and dwindled from day to day . . . I
didn't want to die before my time.   My youth
cried for life, my heart dreamed of blooming . . .
And I awoke from my dream and saw my clothes
hanging rotten on the wall.

*[She hides her head in Abram's embrace, her
body convulsing with sobs.]*

FAYGE.

Children, Faive will be here any moment.

PESHKE.

Rather than realize too late what's going on,
it's far better to —

FAYGE.

[Interrupts her.]

Don't curse yourself, my darling.   You're still
young.   As for me, there's nothing left but sorrow
. . . I'm afraid Faive will come.

PESHKE.

Let him come.   Let him step all over me !

ABRAM.

Nobody under the sun should let another step all over him. I'd resist my own father in such a case !

PESHKE.

[*Draws him close to her, and kisses him softly.*]
No . . . No . . . You're wrong. My mother abandoned me . . . abandoned me . . . She ought this very moment to rise up from her grave with the shards on her eyes, and not leave me behind, alone. She didn't want to quarrel with father . . .
[*Weeps. They remain in embrace.*]

ABRAM.
[*Wipes his eyes.*]

FAYGE.

Don't cry. Don't cry. People who can see the light shouldn't cry . . . I've seen mothers whose cheeks became yellow because they cried too much in their young days. Spots were left . . . Lifelong spots. . .

PESHKE.

No yellow spots will stain my cheeks, granny.

FAYGE.

Abie, you support your mother. Your mother loves you. When you have a mother to love you,

that's enough for anyone. . . I'ts enough to rest
one's head in a mother's bosom. It makes it
easier for both. Even in the grave mothers suffer.
No rest is theirs . . . Their woe is unending . . .

PESHKE.
*[Kisses Abram, puts her arms around his
neck. They stand for a time in embrace.
Silence. Peshke then signals for Abram
to leave. Then aloud.]*

Father will soon come.

*[She goes to the stove. Looks at Abram with
suffering on her features.]*

FAYGE.
Who is that crying in the stillness ? Who is it ?

ABRAM.
[Controls himself, nods to Peshke.]
Good evening. I may step in again tonight.
[Remains for a while at the door.]

FAYGE.
Good luck to you, Abram.

PESHKE.
[Stands near the stove, distraught.]

ABRAM.

[*Goes slowly out, keeping his gaze on Peshke. Silence.*]

FAYGE.

Hu, hu . . . Cold . . . Ah, Youth, Youth ! . . . Beautiful, sunny Youth ! . . . [*After a pause.*] Peshke, you're hungry. Start a fire in the stove.

PESHKE.

No, granny, I'm not hungry.

FAYGE.

I can tell by the trembling of your voice.

PESHKE.

Really, granny, I'm not hungry.

FAYGE.

Youth ! . . . Hu, hu . . . Beautiful, sunny Youth! . . . [*An oppressive silence.*]

FAIVE.

[*Enters. He is frozen. Places on the table a small part of a loaf of black bread. Paces to and fro.*]

FAYGE.

Is that Faive ?

FAIVE.

[*Silent. Sits down by the table, his head resting on his hand.*]

PESHKE.

[*Looks at Faive from where she stands, near the stove.*]

FAYGE.

[*Arising.*]

Faive ? You just came, didn't you ? Peshke, that was your father, wasn't it ?

PESHKE.

Yes

FAYGE.

Make the fire, Peshke. Did you bring anything, Faive ? You must be hungry . . . Peshke hasn't had a bite, either.

FAIVE.

There's bread on the table.

FAYGE.

Bread — bread . . . Of what use is it when . . . There may be plenty of bread, but . . .

FAIVE.

I beg you, mother, let me rest a little.

FAYGE.

Your mother's blind eyes hurt. Your mother's old heart grieves . . . Your young life is fading away . . . And Peshke is a shadow.

PESHKE.

Don't worry about me, granny.

FAYGE.

True, you've brought bread . . . If only you had brought with it a smiling face — a couple of cheerful words . . . Hu, hu. It's cold . . . Without these bread is poison.

FAIVE.

Don't torture me with your words, mother !

FAYGE.

There's bread on the table. Why don't you eat ? [*She goes over to Faive and puts her hands on his shoulders.*] You're silent . . . You don't speak a word . . . That frightens me most of all . . . Why are you both silent ? A house with people in it, and not a word . . . It's hard to bear silence in a house where there are people. [*Takes a few steps back*.] I beg you, look cheerful. Don't degrade the bread . . . A table is an altar, and the bread is its holy sacrifice . . . Don't degrade it . . .

FAIVE.
[Looks at his mother with anger in his eyes.]

FAYGE.
You answer nothing . . . I don't know what I can say to you . . . I can't imagine what's on your mind . . . When you curse, I understand . . . When you beat, I feel what is the matter . . . But when you don't utter a sound . . . One thing, though, — don't you pour out your sea of troubles on the head of your poor Peshke ! She has enough. Peshke ! Where are you ? *[Goes over to Faive and caresses him.]* Vent it all on me, on me !

FAIVE.
[Hides his head in his arms.]

FAYGE.
Your heart is more grieved than usual. Spare your child . . . Let her take her own way . . . Faive, confide in me . . . I'm your mother . . . Remember, when you were a child, how I used to hold you in my lap. I bathed you in my tears. And there in my lap you would laugh and cry. Tell me now, too, what ails you. I'll listen, as I used to then. I'll listen gladly . . . And if I'll be able, I'll weep with my blind eyes . . .

FAIVE.
[*Suddenly arises, and cries out, his features
distorted with pain.*]
Mamma ! Mamma !
[*Remains standing, with head bowed.*]

FAYGE.
[*In a tremulous voice.*]
That's how you cried when I could still see you,
long ago, — when I cradled you in my arms . . .
Speak on . . . Speak on . . . You couldn't say more
than "mamma" then . . . you couldn't . . . Speak,
speak on !

FAIVE.
[*Controls himself. Takes a deep breath.*]
N-no. I can't . . .
[*He leaves.*]

FAYGE.
Whither are you taking your sorrows, my child !
[*Remains standing in the middle of the room.*]

PESHKE.
[*Rushes out into the street and comes back
directly.*]

FAYGE.
Who's that ?

PESHKE.

It's I.

> [*Silence. Finds a rope, and while the old
> woman is speaking, throws it around the
> pipes which lead from the small iron stove
> to the chimney, near the door to the second
> room. With trembling hands she makes a
> noose.*]

FAYGE.

The bread lies on the table, accursed. The sea
of sorrow has been poured out upon it . . . It is
sprinkled with gall . . . Who can touch it ? . . .
Who can think of eating now ? It seems as if the
walls are crumbling about my head . . . Peshke,
what are you doing ?

PESHKE.

I'm dreaming, granny.

FAYGE.

And what are you dreaming, my darling ?

PESHKE.

I'm dreaming that life is easier and happier.
> [*She falls upon the old woman's neck.*]

FAYGE.

My child, you're trembling.

PESHKE.

[*Kisses Fayge.*]

I'm dreaming, granny . . .

FAYGE.

[*Kisses Peshke.*]

What are you dreaming, darling ?

PESHKE.

That my youth won't always be as wretched
as now.

[*Both remain in embrace. Silence.*]

FAYGE.

Why is your heart pounding so, my child ?
Strong, yet restless ?

PESHKE.

From gladness, granny.

[*Silence. Peshke releases herself from the old
woman. She goes on tip-toe to the table and
begins to turn down the light of the lamp
slowly, so that Fayge shall not notice it.*]

FAYGE.

[*Stands in the middle of the cellar. Speaks as if to herself.*]

The light's dying out . . . The light's dying out . . . Dying out . . .

SLOW CURTAIN